Fungicide/Algaecide for Home & Garden Inside & Out

Consan Triple Action 20

Consan Triple Action 20 is a multi-function indoor/outdoor fungicide, algaecide, mildewcide, disinfectant, deodorizer and sanitizer for home and garden.

Completely water soluble as well as biodegradable, CONSAN is labeled and EPA registered for use outside your home for disease control on ornamental plants, grasses and trees, and inside your home for nearly everything that needs to be sanitized, disinfected or deodorized.

Consan Triple Action 20 is an EPA registered product and must be used in accordance with its labeling. Please follow all instructions carefully, use appropriate safety precautions, and wear recommended safety clothing as instructed on the product label

Makes Water Wetter!

Water-In®

Some waters have a hard "skin" of surface tension that prevents that water from penetrating compacted soils. It's that same surface tension that allows a paperclip to float on water!

WATER-IN breaks that surface tension allowing water to move freely into the soil profile allowing less water to be more effective.

Uniform water penetration yields healthier plant growth through more efficient water usage.

Brandt Consolidated, Inc.
2935 South Koke Mill Road
Springfield, Illinois 62711
www.brandtconsolidated.com
Ph. 866-537-5358
Fax. 281-655-1202

Endorsed by Randy Lemmon on Gardenline

1001 GardenLine Questions

Front and Back Photos by
Julie Nanni
www.photographictechniques.com

1001 GardenLine Questions

Randy Lemmon

Publisher: Randy Lemmon

ISBN 978-0-557-96970-8

This book is dedicated to my family

Specifically to my wife Yvonne who gets my passion for both my radio show and my writing. To my son Randal, I hope your love for words leads you to an equal love for writing. To my daughter Selena, while you may be in pre-school today, I think you too will have this family's enthusiasm for the written word.

This book is dedicated to my family

Acknowledgements

There is not enough space here to thank all the people for helping make *1001 GardenLine Questions* a reality. But I'm still going to try.

For starters, thanks to my Friday morning men's group at Community of Faith in Cypress. I think if they did not encourage me to move forward, I probably would still be sitting on the idea of *1001 GardenLine Question.*

Yes, it has come to fruition 8 months later than I projected, but because of their supportive prodding (and of course some timely sarcasm on my delays) it really did happen quicker.

Thanks to Ron Williams, Bill Murff and Kevin Capps, owners of independent Ace Hardware stores in the Houston area, and friends to boot. I can't remember whether it was a group idea or an edict from this select group that planted the seed that became this book. Obviously, the entire Ace Hardware group in this area deserves a huge thanks for their financial backing, or this book never makes it to the printer. They also need to be thanked for just being such great supporters of what I do on GardenLine in the first place.

A very special thanks must go to Ronne Senick once again. Those who know my second book all too well, recognize that name. She's the neighbor across the street that also serves as the editor of the books. Plus, she did this one under an intense deadline pressure. It was not one put on her by me, rather her need to be in California for the birth of her first grandchild and yet still got me the much needed corrections just in time. She couldn't have been more precise and timely considering all the circumstances.

The biggest thanks goes to go to the listeners of the GardenLine radio program – especially those who sent in the hundreds upon hundreds of email questions that made this book a reality. In hindsight, I wished I had saved more of these questions years earlier. I know to keep all of them now, as I see a way to provide (in book form) this never-ending stream of new gardening questions from which we can all learn.

Also, while they really have nothing to do with the book, I still have to thank my Producer Extraordinaire (Behind the Bullet Proof Glass), Kurt Grabenstein (a.k.a. K-Grabs) and Marketing Bottomless Pit, Robert Reese. These two guys make my job so much fun and easier every day that I can't wait to get up every Saturday and Sunday morning to do my job. That excitement also spills over in my desire to write the newsletters, email tips and of course the books.

Randy Lemmon

Introduction

Welcome to **1001 GardenLine Questions**. First, in the matter of full disclosure, there are not 1001 questions in this book. There are only 568! But doesn't **1001 GardenLine Questions** sound and look much better in the title than 568? And if you really want to count the questions, remember there may be two, three and four questions in many of the individual email questions. Plus, I ask several questions myself in many of the lists and discussions at the end of certain chapters.

My estimation is that 90% of this book is new information not covered in my previous two gardening books. There are obvious sections where I pulled information from the most recent book and attached it to the end of specific chapters. A good example would be the 1st chapter in this book on Trees. All the questions and answers are new, but we included standard information at the end like Deep Root Feeding and Planting Techniques from the last book.

But let me be the first to tell you that I actually had more fun writing this book than my previous two. The main goal was to make sure we covered a whole bunch of questions that weren't covered in the two books that I penned before this one.

What's also a lot of fun about this book, was reminding myself of the advice I had written via email to all of these questions over the last couple of years, and to see possibly how some of that advice may have changed. I'm also looking forward to meeting those people whose questions are legitimately in this book at the book signings that will ensue.

To give you another idea of how much fun this book was to write, I can't wait to start working on another book next spring. The question I have to answer is "will it be 2002 GardenLine Questions, or a specific subject matter such as fruits and vegetables or tropical gardening?" Ultimately, I think all the owners of this book and the listeners of GardenLine will help determine that path. Because while I could only answer roughly a thousand questions (okay, 568) in this setting, it could prove another book with another thousand different question could be on the horizon.

So, if after reading this book, you enjoyed it enough to ask further questions and want more of this, then send an email with your proposed book question to the email listed below.

Randy Lemmon

Email future questions at the email link at
www.RandyLemmon.com

Table of Contents

Chapter 1

Trees

Includes:

Top Trees List

Planting Guide

Deep Root Feeding Guide

Q: Can a Bay Leaf tree that is in a pot be transplanted into the ground right now? (September) Irene, Houston

A: Indeed it can be and should be planted in the ground right now. This will allow a couple of months of root development and ensure its survivability during the winter months and thus reward you with ample bay leaves in the spring and summer. Plant in a slightly raised bed for drainage purposes and either incorporate ample rose soil and your planting medium or mix the existing soil with a permanent soil amendment.

Q: I really like Japanese Red Maples, and while I know these are hard to grow here, I bought one anyway. I really want to plant it about 3-4 feet from a foundation. Is this a dumb idea, and did I make a huge mistake in getting a Japanese Red Maple? Gregg, Houston

A: As long as you get the right variety, like Bloodgood, Japanese Red Maples are not all that difficult to grow in Houston. The key to success is shade. They are a true "understory" tree and as such require way more shade than sun. Filtered light all day is okay, but never allow the right varieties for this area to get hammered by direct sunlight. Other varieties known to work in Houston are Burgandy Lace, Emperor, Waterfall and Shiana.

Q: I have a Norfolk Island Pine which I've had for over 20 years. It was very small when I first got it, and it's still in a pot all these years later. But after this freeze (January 2010) it got really singed. Can I just cut off the burned tips? Will this ever look good again? Mary, Brenham

A: In the Brenham area, consider yourself lucky that it's still alive. Many Norfolk Island Pines were killed by the January freeze; especially any of those not near the coast. You can prune back the tips, but also be prepared to prune any green limbs as well, because if you don't prune to the shape or integrity of the normal growth, it may never look "right" again. These semi-tropical plants were never intended to be pruned.

Q: What fertilizer do you recommend to use on Crape Myrtles, to promote more flowering? Celeste, Magnolia

A: Almost anything! Seriously, Crapes will feed on just about anything. There are several Crape Myrtle-specific foods on the market, but as a general rule rose food, and any 1-2-1 ratio fertilizer will work. That's why 12-24-12 type fertilizers have long been a staple feeding of crapes over the years. Even then, there are a number of specific Crape Myrtle Foods on the market by names like Nelson's Nutri Star for Crape Myrtles and Carl Pool's Crape Myrtle Food.

Q: Randy, I took your advice on the pruning of crape myrtles this year, and did not do near as much as I have in the past. Should I start feeding regularly now (March) or wait until the blooming time? Arte, Porter

A: Yes, you should feed regularly starting in March/April. Then you can feed every two months if you use the slow release types (as noted earlier) or the rose-type foods you can feed once a month. Never wait until blooming time.

Q: We are looking for a palm tree that will not grow beyond 12 feet. I want to plant it in the ground by our pool. Do you have any recommendations? Is there anything other than sago palms? David, The Woodlands

A: Even though they are not the most cold-hardy palm, I say it's a moral imperative to have Dwarf Pygmy Date Palms as an accent to a pool. Granted I lost mine to the 2010 freeze, but they are so inexpensive and easy to grow that replacing them if the worst happens is not a bank-breaker.

With the multi-trunk growth pattern and their ability to stay less than 10 feet are huge selling points for me. So as not to look too myopic, you can also consider the following palms too. Needle Palm is a good choice, because it maxes out at 10 ft. Mediterranean Palms are good for pools and more cold-hardy but can reach over 15 ft. in several years. Pindo Palms can max out at 15 ft., but they have such a big trunk that doesn't go well with a pool.

Q: What kind of fertilizer should I use for Bald Cypress trees? We have about 5 of them planted on our bayou and I want to keep them as healthy as possible. Donna, Angleton

A: Anything! Seriously, any tree and shrub fertilizer, any organic lawn food, any leftover synthetic lawn food or any azalea food will work. They are not picky, and almost all the aforementioned suggestions are highest in the nitrogen (or first number in the analysis), which is ultimately what they will green up on.

Q: I just saw a tree that I think I must have. My research tells me it is a Vitex. I don't think I've ever heard you mention it before. Is this a plant you like? Will it work well in this area? If I can plant it, can you also tell me how to care for it? Nancy, League City

A: I do like the Vitex (a.k.a. Lavender tree; Chaste tree) a lot, and I admit that maybe I don't give it as much positive feedback as I ought to. But it is a wonderful alternative to crape myrtles in Houston, but without all the color variations. It pretty much comes in purple and purple only. There are some white ones, but they are usually very hard to find. But when they are in full-bloom, they are significantly more striking with their purple bloom spikes than anything else out there. And since we think of them as an alternative to crapes, you can also feed them just like they are crapes and you can prune them late in the winter or early in the spring as well. Thanks for reminding me to keep the Vitex in the forefront of my recommendations again.

Q: What is that fern that is small and grows on the trunk of our oak tree? If it is dry outside it quickly turns brown and seems to go away, but when it rains it's green again. Do you know what this is and if it is a problem we need to take care of? Katie, Winnie

A: What you described is Lichen, which usually shows up on trees in area of high humidity and sparse canopies. What they are is a symbiotic relationship between algae and fungi. The effect is slightly detrimental, meaning if left untreated it could suffocate the tree over a long period of time. But as long as you keep the tree's roots healthy (you should know how I feel about deep root feeding/watering) then the healthier the canopy, the more likely the lichen will fizzle away. Some people have been known to spray the trunk with systemic fungicides, namely Kocide or any Banner-based (PPZ) type of fungicide as well. But this is not a sign of sick tree by definition.

Q: I recently potted up two Phoenix Roebellini palms (Dwarf Pygmy Date Palms). I used Scotts Potting soil. Both have lost a lot of their green, and more yellow shades are appearing every day. Do I need to add something like iron or palm food? Or did I use the wrong soil? Larry, Friendswood.

A: You used the wrong soil, in my opinion. You should never use anything considered Potting Soil for landscape plants/palms. Frankly, Dwarf Pygmy Date Palms are much better suited to a landscape bed, but if you have to keep it in a pot, then you have to use rose soil as your base. You could add iron, and you could add palm food, but the yellowing will either come back or persist because the potting soil is not holding on to the nutrients the palm tree needs for long periods of time. It's simply too porous.

Q: What do you think of the Royal Empress tree (Paulownia)? Is it true they have brighter blooms than any other tree? What should be my concerns? I'm thinking about planting a couple on a golf course lot. Layne, Columbia Lakes

A: Let me answer this with the standard GOOD NEWS vs. BAD NEWS explanation. The good news is that it is a fast-growing tree. It does have beautiful purple/blue flowers and can adapt quite easily to southeast Texas soils. The bad news is that it is fast-growing, and in almost all cases, fast-growing trees tend to have a shorter life span and are susceptible to more insects and diseases. Royal Empress (Paulownia) trees also have invasive root systems to you don't want them near foundations or landscape beds. And finally, while the blooms are beautiful they make a mess on concrete, sidewalks and cars when they fall. Since you want to put them out near a golf course, then I give you a green light.

Q: I have a Water Oak that has been dropping acorns for about 2-3 weeks (September). I've lived here for 15 years and have never had them drop this early. Is this normal? Should I just ignore this, since it's going to shed its leaves in another month or so? Wendell, Cypress

A: It's not abnormal. When a tree, that regularly produces acorns, drops them earlier than you recall, then it's simply a sign of stress. When this question was asked, we were coming off of a drought-stressed summer of 2010. If you couple that with the freeze of January 2010, this tree is probably indicating a double-stress with the early development and drop of acorns. Keep in mind too, that an inordinate amount of acorns is a sure sign that the tree is in need of a deep root watering/feeding program.

Q: Randy, I think I need a root barrier installed in my back yard to protect my foundation and patio. I have a few pine trees with roots slightly on the surface and getting close to my foundation. What's your opinion on these things, and are they worth it? Jim, Spring

A: Let's answer the "is it worth it?" part first. I will warn everyone that "root-barricading" in general is somewhat expensive. But it's like that old car repair commercial "You can pay me now; or you can pay me later!" Foundation repair is way more expensive than root barricading, but are you willing to spend 2000-3000 dollars now or 10,000-15,000 dollars on actual foundation repair later. Remember too, and I don't doubt it's covered in other questions throughout this book, but roots don't do the damage to the foundations. It's the moisture they sap from around and under the foundation that is the true threat. And when a foundation doesn't have ample moisture it breaks. So, in summary: I think root barricading is well worth it not only as a practical control method, but even more so as an insurance policy against even more expensive foundation repairs.

Q: We lost our Arizona Ash tree in our back yard to Ike. I would like to replace it with a fast growing tree (I miss the shade). Someone told me to plant a Drummond Red Maple. I would like it to get fairly large to shade the back yard and the back half of my house. I have a Live Oak in the front of my house and it shades the front half of my house. I would like your opinion on what kind of trees will grow fast and do well in southwest Houston. Tony, SW Houston

A: I do like the Drummond Red Maple for this area. There are several other trees too that work well and will provide shade in a few years. One other that I particularly like these days is the Nuttall Oak.

Q: I've heard that you like certain trees, and I've heard that there are certain trees that should be avoided. I think I have one of those. Can you tell me whether the Silver Leaf Maple is one of them? Sara, Cypress.

A: You are correct, in that the Silver Leap Maple is not a good choice for this area. While it grows fast and has rather unique leaves, it is not long-lived for this area. Because it grows so fast, it is very susceptible to diseases and insect pressures. Once it starts to "decline" it can rarely, if ever, be saved. Another tree I would avoid planting in this area is the Arizona Ash. While Green Ash and White Ash tend to do better for this area, an Arizona Ash also has a limited life span.

Q: I have a Magnolia tree that I bought from a local mass merchandiser, and planted it in my backyard. It has been four years and it has never bloomed. It has grown to about 12 feet tall. Is there anything I can do to get it to bloom? Dana, Houston

A: Often times, when you buy a tree from what I refer to as a mass merchandiser or a big box store, you may not be getting the right variety for our area and they will struggle for several years to acclimate. Both mass merchandisers and big box stores buy from national and regional suppliers and get great price breaks on varieties that may be better suited for northern climates. Thus, they get mass quantities that have to be divvied-up among all their locations, and a tree designed for Tennessee, will be sold in Texas. But, as long as it is still alive there are a couple of things we can try to do to encourage growth. Azalea foods are also designed for Magnolias, and should be used 2-3 times a year. Also, if the tree has grown that little in four years, that could indicate that it wasn't planted correctly. There may be an opportunity here to "re-plant" the tree, in order for the root system to have room to grow. Once you have good roots, you will get lots of new growth. And on a Magnolia, if you get that new growth coupled with the Azalea food, you will likely see your first blooms.

Q: I have a question about my Live Oak trees. They are relatively new trees (planted about 3 years ago) but they are covered with ball-shaped knots all over the trees. They have a small hole or two in each one. Is this something I need to be worried about? Or, is this life-threatening to the tree? If so, what do you recommend for treatment? Karl, Dickinson

Q: I have fuzzy yellow growths on the leaves of my Oak Tree. Is this something to worry about? I've heard it's a gall? What do I treat it with? Raj, Houston

A: I lumped these two question together, because they are both what are referred to as insect galls, which you can research online for more detail if you use those two words – Insect Galls. But in short, they are not a problem, nor are they life-threatening to the trees. These insect galls are simply the tree's way of defending itself from a little intrusion. That intrusion was a beneficial wasp, laying its eggs on a small branch or underside of the leaf of each tree. The bark grows up around the eggs and sort of protects these baby wasp eggs from the elements. Most trees grow out of them. Thus, there is nothing that you need to spray or treat them with. The other fuzzy type will likely cause the leaves to yellow, but again this not life-threatening and not worth treating.

Q: We bought an older home, and the previous owner planted a Live Oak in the backyard about 20 feet from the house. Is this too close? Should the tree be removed before it gets any bigger? Bobby, League City

Q: I have a Pine tree approximately 25 feet tall and approximately 14 feet from the house. Will its root system damage the home foundation? Tim, The Woodlands

A: One rule of thumb I've always had for planting trees is to plant them at a minimum of 20 feet from a foundation. 30 feet is even better and 40 feet would be the best distance. However, when you come into a situation such as this, it may also be worth investing in a root barricading system. There are companies that will put barricade in a few feet from the foundation, so that the roots of the trees never rob the moisture from under the foundation. It is that desiccation from under the foundation that ultimately causes foundation problems. And preventing the problem with a root barricade is much cheaper than fixing a foundation problem later. By the way, if a tree is 10 feet or less from a foundation, simply removing it isn't always a wise choice either. Cutting it down to a stump is the smarter choice. Total removal so close to a foundation, can create such a huge cavity, that it poses a whole other threat to a foundation.

Q: I am extending my driveway with brick. I have 2 big roots about 3 inches round extending above the ground level. Can they be cut without damaging the tree? Keith, Houston

A: Yes and no! You can cut one big root per year on an established tree, but if you cut more than one, you could destabilize the tree. Another factor you need to take into consideration is whether the tree has been deep root watered/fed over the years. Because emerging roots, such as this, are also indicators that the tree is under duress. If you don't get the tree on a deep root care program, it could very well send up big roots year after year looking for moisture. Thus, taking one big root per year would actually become an effort in futility.

Q: Can you tell me how to dig up a Chestnut Oak for transplanting purposes? It's about 8-feet tall and has a 1-inch diameter trunk. Also, can I send it to its new location with bare roots? Gary, Kingwood

A: Let me answer the second question first. No, you cannot send it to its new home bare-rooted. In this region, when you transplant a tree, you need to take as much of the dirt around the root structure as possible. This helps it acclimate to the transplant much better. To transplant, get as much root ball and its dirt as possible. On this size tree I would dig a circle that is 12-16 inches away from the trunk. The larger the trunks, the further out you need to start digging. Then dig down, conically, about 12 inches. The larger the tree, the further down you would need to dig up to 21 inches. You will sever some roots, and that's to be expected. Pull out the tree and its root ball and set it on a tarp. Take the tarp, wrapped around the root ball and move this specimen to its new hole, which will be planted per the tree planting technique also noted in this book.

Q: Would it be okay to do some tree trimming (lower branches only) on some Live Oaks today, with the temperatures expected to be in the 20s and 30s? Mark, North Side

A: We do recommend tree pruning when trees are in their highest state of dormancy, and that's usually the winter time. However, it's not a good idea to prune anything when the temperatures are freezing or below. The fresh cut is like a straw to the cold air, pulling it further into the plant than need be. Again, pruning during the dormant season is recommended, but try to avoid it when the temperatures are that cold.

Q: I want to plant a tree in my front yard because that side of the house faces east. I was thinking of planting a Maple tree, because it gets so full and grows so fast, in order to provide shade. Is that a good tree choice? And, is this a good time of the year (February) to plant it? Adam, League City

A: Be careful in your choice of Maple trees. There are a couple of good choices, such as Drummond Red Maple and the Woodlands Red Maple. But you have to avoid the Silver Leaf Maple, as I've probably alluded to hundreds of times on the radio show. They are short-lived for this area, and always have disease and insect problems. We usually say that as long as the tree is containerized, we can transplant in this region almost any time of the year. I wouldn't do it if the weather is close to freezing and I wouldn't do it when temperatures are in the 100s as well. So, late February is normally a great time to get the root system established before the spring growth.

Q: What is the best fertilizer for Pine trees? Bob, Humble

A: I have found that if you feed Pine trees some Azalea food, they will respond very favorably. They like the acid environment, much like Azaleas, Gardenias and Camellias, so use acid-loving plant foods. And I suggest two feedings with such food; once in the spring and once in the summer. The myriad of organic fertilizers that have Mycorrhizal fungi are also a good option for Pine Trees. You will hear and see the word Mycor, as a shortened version of Mycorrhizal.

Q: Please tell me what you think of the Kwanzan Flowering Cherry tree, and how it compares to the Bradford Pear. Ruby D., La Porte

A: My answer is not about "a comparison" because frankly there is no comparison. The point I would like to make, and that can be applied to almost any tree you hear or read about that you would like to try in this region, is to figure out the recommended zones. We've all seen the growing zones or regions, right? Good for zones 5-9; which is what the Kwanzan says. Here's the problem in almost all cases with questions like these: We really aren't in zone 9. Instead, we are more in the number 10 zone. That means, to me, that it's not the best alternative for this region. Because the further translation is, if it does well in zone 5 (North of Dallas, TX) then our heat and humidity will almost assuredly do a tree like this in. There are exceptions to the rule, but in the case of the Kwanzan versus a Bradford Pear for a flowering ornamental tree, there is no comparison. If you want to avoid the problems of the Bradford, then find the Aristocratic.

Q: This morning, on your radio show, you talked about spraying copper-based fungicides on the crown of Queen Palms. I'm in Port O'Connor and have some Foxtail Palms that have survived the freeze, but I don't want to lose them to anything else. Is it worth spraying them with the fungicide you recommended?

A: The copper-based fungicide treatment is recommended for almost any palm tree where it's obviously still alive following the harsh January 2010 freeze, but as an insurance policy of the new growth that might be fragile trying to re-emerge. So, yes, you can use it on the crown of Foxtail palms as well. Let me be the first to admit that while there is not concrete research date on this, the theory behind such fungal treatments is to control damaging pathogens that lead to bud rot (the bud on a palm is known as the apical meristem). The most famous of all the copper-based fungicides is Kocide.

Top Trees for the Gulf Coast

The most obvious question I get has to be, "What is the fastest growing shade tree?" What hasn't changed from the first book is that there is no one "silver bullet" or "foolproof" answer. That's because everyone has different requirements in terms of space and soil conditions. This is also why I keep revising what used to be my Top Ten List. It was a Top Dozen a few years ago, and has now grown to a Top 14 Trees for Houston and the Gulf Coast. The Live Oak is a great choice, and can and should be planted in many landscapes. This list is specific for the 3 requirements always asked of me for tree choices:

1.   They have to be acclimated to the Gulf Coast climate – I assume that would go without saying.

2.   Gives us the best chance at the shortest time for an ample shade tree.

3.   Something that is readily available at reputable nurseries and tree farms along the Gulf Coast.

Top Trees

1. Laurel Oak -- (Quercus laurifolia)

2. Green Ash – (Fraxinus penssylvanica)

3. Nuttall Oak – (Quercus nattallii)

4. Shumard Red Oak – (Quercus shumardii)

5. White Ash -- (Fraxinus Americana)

6. Overcup Oak – (Quercus lyrata)

7. Drummond Red Maple – (Acer rubrum)

8. Mexican Sycamore – (Plantanus mexicanus

9. Monterrey Oak -- (Quercus polymorphus

10. Camphor -- (Cinnamomum camphora

11. Cedar Elm – (Ulmus crassifolia

12. Corky Winged Elm – (Imus alata)

13. Bur Oak - (Quercus macrocarpa)

14. Water Oak – (Quercus nigra)

Randy's Planting Technique for Trees (& Large Shrubs)

For every tree suggested in this gardening guide, the true secret to success is in how they are planted. In other words, successful root develop is the ultimate way to have a successful shade tree establish in your landscape. Most people, who aren't educated to the gardening foibles along the Gulf Coast, usually dig a hole the size of the root ball of their new tree and slide the tree into the hole. With our preponderance of clay, that is something of a prison sentence to the root ball of that tree.

I have a technique I call "Twice As Wide & Half Again As Deep". If you follow this technique, you are doing everything you can to ensure that the root systems of a newly planted tree has some room in which to establish itself. Many people have found, just digging a hole and popping in a tree's root ball doesn't always work. That's because, in most cases, the hole is dug just big enough for the root ball. Consequently, the roots are immediately faced with the need to penetrate the hard clay soil. So, the tree stagnates and doesn't seem to grow much at all. That's why I call it a prison sentence as opposed to a death sentence. By the way, this technique that we use for trees also works for large shrubs as well.

While most landscape plants should be planted in raised beds, trees will actually do just fine in "existing soil" if we just give them a helping hand. Some folks dig more accommodating large holes, but, they backfill with peet, humus, mulch or even fluffy potting soil mixes. That normally leads to an area that's continually too wet, so, the root system can't breath and the tree yellows and dies. So, the tree planting maxim I've tried to live by is to help the tree properly adjust to the existing soil conditions. Since clay isn't really a very good environment, we have to add a permanent soil amendment. There are a few examples of soil amendments listed a bit later.

Here's where the "Twice As Wide & Half Again As Deep" technique comes into play. First, dig a hole two to three times wider than the root ball, and half-again the depth of the actual root ball. For example, if the container is 10 inches across and 10 inches deep, you will need a hole 20-30 inches across and 15 inches deep. When you dig the dirt out of the hole, throw the dirt on a drop cloth or tarp as you dig. Next, add the permanent soil amendment to the dirt you've dug out. Every amendment has different dirt-to-amendment ratios, but you're almost always safe at 6-to-1 or 5-to-1 dirt-to-amendment.

Add enough of this mixture to the bottom of the hole so that when the tree is inserted, the top of the root ball is at ground level or even just ever so slightly raised, so that it's 1-inch above the soil line. You will need to tamp down the mixture in that "half-again" as deep part so that there won't be any air pockets. Then, center the tree in the hole, and fill in around the ball, tamping down continuously as you go. Don't worry about "compacting" the area ... the permanent soil amendment you've added will essentially keep the soil aerated.

Finally, build a mulch ring on top, and water in. In fact, water once a week for the first year of the tree's life. As the tree's roots acclimate to their new environment, they'll strengthen enough to penetrate the harder clay soil beyond the zone you established. Again, the whole intention is to give the tree a head start towards acclimating to existing soil conditions. Thus, if we can make the first year or two easier on the roots with the looser soil/amendment mixture, then the easier it is for the healthier roots to penetrate the hard clay soil when it reaches it again.

Permanent Soil Amendments

Commercial Names

Tru-Gro (kiln-fired rocks, a concrete by-product)

Schultz Soil Conditioner

Fertilome Natural Guard Soil Conditioner

Non-Commercial (homemade) Alternatives

Small pea gravel (the smallest you can find)

Pure clay kitty litter

Granular gypsum (pelletized gypsum)

Haydite (crushed granite)

Deep Root Feeding of Trees

In our clay soils, tree roots are often in search of moisture and nutrients. When roots detect nothing, in terms of moisture, down deep (where they prefer to be) they search near the soil surface. Then, they buckle sidewalks and cause mower-mayhem all over lawns. At least once every hour on GardenLine, I probably hammer home the importance of deep-root watering and feeding trees.

Listeners call because their trees haven't grown much since they planted them two years ago. Or they call about the roots of older trees coming out of the ground. These are examples of trees in dire need of deep-root watering and feeding. The key is in developing holes in the earth above the root system that go down 18 inches. They can be developed with a Ross Root Feeder, a soil auger, a post-hole digger, or a tool you've designed yourself using something like a piece of steel rebar.

The bigger the holes, the fewer you will need. With smaller holes, like those made with tools like the Ross Root Feeder, the more you will need. If the holes are bigger than an inch in diameter, however, you will need to fill them with pea gravel or organic matter like mulch or compost. Smaller holes, Mother Nature fills gradually and naturally. With the holes in place, nature and your watering system will provide plenty of moisture to trickle down the holes. However, I do recommend organic foods from time to time, to aid in the natural microbial breakdown. You don't have to water each individual hole. The same holds true for feeding, but if your holes are two inches in diameter or more (like post-hole size), you can soak those areas individually with organic foods or soil activators. With small holes, soak the entire area with a spray-on organic liquid. Or, use compost over the surface to slowly work its way down. I truly mean this: ANY ORGANIC FOOD WILL DO when feeding trees. To me, as long as it says "organic" I don't care whether it's liquid or granular in form. Refer to our Lawn Care Chapter and the organic schedule to see names of all the organic foods I endorse.

Additional Deep Root Feeding Tips

- Remember that your holes need to be both inside and outside the drip line. Start them at least two feet from the trunk of the tree.

- Remember how tree roots grow. Often, we picture them growing only laterally, but they will actually grow down in well-watered, organic soils.

- Remember that this process must be consistent. Even healthy mature trees will benefit from deep-root watering and feeding.

Words of Warning:

- Just feeding with granular synthetic food actually eats up beneficial microbes that we want to increase down in the root zone. That's why I emphasize using organic foods for the roots of trees. Yes, you will get some green up with synthetic tree foods, but your overall goal should be healthier soils.

- If you're auguring with a drill bit bigger than two inches, it's wise to have gas, phone and other utility lines marked prior to drilling.

- Don't forget to add additional holes outside the "drip line" as the tree matures.

- Hire a tree service company if you think this is too much work.

Chapter 2

Shrubs

Q: I saw you on a local TV show, where you talked about the yellow Knock Out rose. Did I hear you correctly, that you thought it smelled like Plumeria? I love yellow roses, in general, and would like to know if these are really worth investing in? Sherry, Spring

A: Yes, I truly believe the yellow Knock Out smells like a standard plumeria fragrance. But there is a big "BUT' in this scenario. They don't bloom nearly as prolific as the red or pink Knock Outs. My guess is that this is a "work in progress" and one day they will have those producing blooms on a grander scale, but as for now they truly struggle to re-bloom after the first flush usually produced in a greenhouse setting. So, hold off for another year or so, and then I'll tell you whether they are worth investing in long-term.

Q: What fertilizer do you recommend to use on crape myrtles, to promote more flowering? Celeste, Magnolia

A: Almost anything! Seriously, Crapes will feed on just about anything. There are several crape myrtle-specific foods on the market, but as a general rule rose food, and any 1-2-1 ratio fertilizer will work. That's why 12-24-12 type fertilizers have long been a staple feeding of crapes over the years. Even then, there are a number of specific Crape Myrtle Foods on the market by names like Nelson's Nutri Star for Crape Myrtles and Carl Pool's Crape Myrtle Food.

Q: Randy, I took your advice on the pruning of crape myrtles this year, and did not do near as much as I have in the past. Should I start feeding regularly now (March) or wait until the blooming time? Arte, Porter

A: Yes, you should feed regularly starting in March/April. Then you can feed every two months if you use the slow release types (as noted earlier) or the rose-type foods you can feed once a month. Never wait until blooming time.

Q: Randy, I want to plant a Duranta plant. What do you think of this plant? We also live in the Heights, if that makes any difference? Jay, Heights

A: I love the Duranta, also known as Golden Dewdrop. In my last book, I have it recommended as one of the Top 30 landscape shrubs for this area. It has beautiful purple/blue blooms many months of the year, and can be shaped or left to grow in an arching/weeping pattern. My only warning to you, especially in the Heights, is to make sure it gets ample sun. This is by no means a shade loving plant.

Q: I keep missing the name of the plant which you say smells so good. Can you please tell that name? I think it has something like Almond in it. Karen, Houston

A: Sweet Almond Verbena! It may not be the most beautiful plant but it really packs a great aroma. And everyone has a different opinion of what that smell reminds them. To me, it smells like grape soda, but not as much as Texas Mountain Laurel does. However, Sweet Almond Verbena gives you that awesome aroma many more months out of the year than Texas Mountain Laurel.

Q: I have a Sweet Almond Verbena on my deck in a pot. It seems to only do well if I water it every day. Does this plant really like a lot of water or would it be better if I planted it in the ground? Kevin, Humble

A: The Sweet Almond Verbena will drink the water in a potted situation, because it has such a dense mass of roots that require a lot of moisture. To me, it's more important about where I want the plant since it smells so good when it's in bloom. I'm willing to water mine daily because I want them by the back door for that fragrance. However, as you noted, it probably would be best for the plant long-term if it was planted in the ground. And much like a palm tree with a dense root system only two feet away from the trunk, once established, it will require much less water.

Q: Our large, well-established, split-leaf philodendrons shed all their leaves after the freeze. The trunks are about 6 ft. tall -- a bit overgrown for their spot. The plants don't appear to be damaged other than the leaves. Can we cut the trunks back? How much? When? Lee Ann, Seabrook

A: After the Blizzard of '09 and the harsh freezes of January '10, many tropicals such as Lee Ann's Split-Leaf suffered serious damage for the first time in years. The good news in many cases such as Lee Ann's is that it's obvious there are still plenty of healthy trunks, but the leaves/fronds are goners. Yes, you can and should cut back the trunk to help encourage new growth later in the spring/summer. How much is up to you, but likely more than half, because leaving too-tall trunks with no leaves will look awkward. And as long as you are convinced there are no more freezes, that's the "when" part of Lee Ann's questions.

Q: Is a Japanese Blueberry tree good for the Katy area? I have a 15 ft. circle area next to a pool to plant a tree. I need something that grows fast, gives me shade in the late evening, but won't shed a lot of leaves in to the pool. Any ideas on what might work? Steven, Katy

A: I like the way you're thinking. A Japanese Blueberry (a.k.a. Elyocarpus) is a great choice for that area. However, you may want to find a really nice sized one right away for the shade purposes. Because while they can get to 20 feet in under 5 years, the first two years you will have no shade with a baby-sized one to begin with. Another evergreen option for you to consider that can be shaped into a small tree is Texas Wax Myrtle.

Q: I just saw a shrub/tree that I think I must have. My research tells me it is a Vitex. I don't think I've ever heard you mention it before. Is this a plant you like? Will it work well in this area? If I can plant it, can you also tell me how to care for it? Nancy, League City

A: I do like the Vitex (a.k.a. Lavender tree; Chaste tree) a lot, and I admit that maybe I don't give it as much positive feedback as I ought to. But it is a wonderful alternative to crape myrtles in Houston, but without all the color variations. It pretty much comes in purple and purple only. There are some white ones, but they are usually very hard to find. But when they are in full-bloom, they are significantly more striking with their purple bloom spikes than anything else out there. And since we think of them as an alternative to crapes, you can also feed them just like they are crapes and you can prune them late in the winter or early in the spring as well. Thanks for reminding me to keep the Vitex in the forefront of my recommendations again.

Q: My Sago palm has a very large cone, but no new growth. My other Sago palm has new growth like normal. Do you have any suggestions? Gerry, Pasadena

A: Once that male seed cone starts to tilt and whither a bit, then just yank it or cut it off and you will more than likely start to see new fronds emerging. Sagos are either male or female, and you can tell which by the seed head they grow. Males are like yours with long cylindrical pine cone-like structures. Female seed heads are more spread out and filled with orange to brown seeds the size of walnuts. In both cases, new growth will begin once the seed head has run its course. But in most cases, it is best to remove all that you can to encourage new frond growth.

Q: When is the best time to cut off the yellowing fronds of my Sago palm? The new growth began a month ago, but didn't I hear you say something about not pruning palm fronds until new growth comes out? Mark, Houston

A: You did hear that correctly. Here are a couple of simple rules that apply to most palms (Yes, I know a sago is a cycad, but we treat it just as if it were a real palm). You can prune off yellow fronds whenever you want, if you have plenty of green fronds. What you heard me discuss was following the January 2010 freeze, we leave all palm fronds in place that are yellow or brown, until the new growth has lain out. In your case, the new fronds have lain out, and you can prune the yellow growth back. If the new growth was just emerging, I would have advised waiting. You should never leave a palm frond-less, by pruning off everything, until you see the growth lying out.

Q: I am looking for a fast-growing hedge to use as a fence. I would like them to be 15 ft. or more in the first few years. Is this possible? If so, what do you recommend? Ron, Conroe

A: This is an easy one. I'll bet many GardenLine faithful know the answer to this. Texas Wax Myrtle! Also known as Southern Wax Myrtle, is a native plant that can reach 15 feet in the first three years after planting. Plus, they are impervious to most diseases and insect pressures. If there's one drawback, it's that they have to be pruned for shape at least once a year.

Q: I have a ficus tree about 20 feet tall, growing right near a large lake. It lost all its leaves after the freeze (January 2010). It has yet to put out any new growth. How do I know whether to give up on it or not? Is it time to take it out? Is there any chance it will come back? Michael, Seabrook.

A: You simply have to scrape the bark of the trunk with a pocket knife, and see if there's any green in the wood. A ficus that wasn't protected, and out in the open like yours, is probably dead. But do the test, and if there is green at this time of the year (April), then you have a fighting chance. No green – no life!

Q: I have an Oleander question. I planted 10 along a fence. They flower nicely in the spring, but the flowers diminish through the summer. From August on, they grow lush and green, but have no flowers. How do I get more flowers out of them during the summer? Is there anything special I should be feeding them? Tom, Sugarland

A: Let's start with the very last part of the question. If you aren't feeding them anything, then by all means start feeding them something. The fun part of Oleanders is that they will feed on almost anything. Experts have recommended Rose Food for years. I've seen some of the healthiest Oleanders in yards that use nothing by high end compost as a top dressing and ultimately its food. Just make sure you avoid high nitrogen fertilizers, or anything with the first number the highest in the analysis.

Q: All my plants are in pots/containers. I need to re-pot a yellow bell plant right now (Esperanza). But I hear you talking about different soils for indoor plants versus outdoor ones and different soils you like in general. Should I use rose soil for this or should I use the Lady Bug Natural Vortex potting soil you seem to like for potted plants? Cindy, Houston

A: For an outdoor plant like the Esperanza, I would use a high quality rose soil. I prefer high quality potting soils, such as the Vortex you mentioned, mostly for indoor, tropical and hanging basket situations.

Q: I have several Gardenias that are loaded with blooms each spring, but very few seem to open. What can I do about this? Vernon, Houston

A: I wouldn't doubt that somewhere else in all the answers to all the questions I get that this answer can be applied again and again – It's all about consistency! I'm talking about consistency of moisture, consistency of food (they love azalea food) and with Gardenias consistency of light to filtered light. But there is one thing that will keep Gardenia blooms from opening and that's a lack of humidity in the area. That touches back on the consistency of moisture aspect. If all else is normal, then try upping the humidity in the area by slightly increasing the moisture this year.

Q: I have an Evergreen Wisteria (Millettia reticulate) vine that is currently producing seed pods. I would love to preserve the seeds for future planting. What is your advice? Mary, Tomball

A: I like the way you're thinking. Propagation of Wisteria through seed pods is a no-brainer. You simply wait for the seed pod to start drying and as soon as it looks like it's going to crack open, put a lunch sack around it, clip off the seed pod and store the seeds until spring. Then, you can experiment with the seed propagation all you want in early spring. Try different types of soil from potting soil to rose soil and you could have a veritable Wisteria farm on your hands. People have been known to sow such seed pods directly into flower beds following the final frost of early spring.

Q: I have been seeing a plant around lately that is beautiful, purple version of what I might call Pampas Grass. It has purple leaf plumes and the soft, feathery tufts at the top just like Pampas Grass. Do you know what this is? Linda, Houston

A: Give yourself a hand. You did a great job of describing Purple Fountain Grass. It is readily available in the Houston market, and as you already noted, is quite beautiful when growing well. I've developed this love/hate relationship with Purple Fountain Grass. I love the color too, and I'm a huge proponent of landscape grasses such as this. However, since this is one of the less cold-hardy landscape grasses, it struggles to come back after harsh winters in this region. If we have a mild winter, you're really going to love them.

Q: Which variety of Lorapetalum stays mostly burgundy in color during the summer months? Jeff, Houston

A: You would think that there is only one simple variety to prescribe that answers this question. Alas, there are way too many varieties to list. Nevertheless, the one that I know works the best and keeps its color the longest is known as Plum Delight. Oh, by the way, as long as you keep them in well-drained beds, and feed them with Azalea food, almost all Lorapetalums will give you dark burgundy leaves year-round.

Q: I have several large Lorapetalum plants that need to be pruned. If I prune them now, (November) will they still bloom this coming spring? Is there a better time of the year to prune them, or does it really matter? Lynn, Houston

A: This is a tough call, because I sense you really need to prune them for size right now. And while you can prune them at almost any time of the year, you're right to be worried about cutting into the bloom. Normally, I always recommend major pruning of Lorapetalums after the first spring bloom. But, if you're willing to forego the blooms this spring, you can prune them back by one-third today.

Q: When can I transplant such tropical plants such as Esperanza, Hibiscus and Sago Palms? Is now a good time (November) or should I wait until spring? Anthony, Orange

A: I would wait until spring on these particular plants. You may have heard or read from me that October-November is a great time to do landscape work. And that is still the case for containerized plants, but moving an existing tropical this close to the winter months, is probably a death sentence. When it comes to tropicals that need to be moved, I always consider April through June the best possible time.

Q: We have Asian Jasmine ground cover in both the front and back yard. The front yard is not doing as well as the back. The front gets plenty of sunlight, while the back gets more shade. There's a sprinkler system on both. What do you think is the problem? Holly, The Woodlands

A: At first thought, and without the benefit testing the soil in both cases, I would have to say it's too much sun. Asian Jasmine is an all-purpose plant, and can and does do well in both sunlight and shade. Thus, where almost everything is the same in terms of soil, moisture, and food, then it tells me the light requirements are in play. Remember too, that while Asian Jasmine seems to be an all-purpose plant, it does do better in filtered light to shade.

Q: My question is about planting Crape Myrtles in the heat of the summer (July/August). Yea or Nay? We got great deals on them from the nursery having a 70% Off Sale, but can you tell us whether to keep it in the container until next spring or plant it now? Rell, Missouri City

A: Plant them now, if you can baby them for the next couple of months with watering. If you're going to go on vacation the rest of the summer, don't plant them until you get back. I love the idea of getting great deals in the heat of the summer from our local nurseries and garden centers. Those 50%-75% Off Sales are worth checking out. Just remember to get such sale items in the ground by November so they establish their root systems to carry them through the winter. Then, an autumn-established root system will reward you with ample growth come spring time.

Q: I sprayed a shrub with wasp spray. I hosed it down with water for about 5 minutes after I killed the wasps. Did I kill the shrub? Did I do the right thing with the water right after? Rick, Houston

A: What Rick did is a common problem. The issue is that most wasp and hornet sprays are oil-based and that oil along with the insecticidal property coats the leaves of the plant in question. This will probably defoliate the section where the oil was sprayed, but it isn't likely to kill the plant. Rick also did the right thing by trying to rinse it off, immediately thereafter. Unfortunately, it only takes that oil a few seconds to do its damage.

Q: I have a front yard bed of Red Berry Hollies that are not growing much. Is this a good time (September) to re-work the beds? If not, when is the best time of the year? Plus, what fertilizer do these plants prefer? By the way these are the hollies where the leaves do not stick you all that bad. Sheryl, Pearland

A: You're probably talking about Needle Point Hollies. Actually the month of October is considered the best month for landscaping work along the Gulf Coast. So, if you can wait just one more month, then you can get busy transplanting or re-working these beds. When you re-work the new beds, just make sure you have plenty of Rose Soil in which to put the root systems. As per your question on feeding -- One of the best "inside secrets" for all Hollies is to feed them with either Azalea food or organic fertilizers that have a high first numbers, such as a 6-2-4 or 8-2-4.

Q: We are looking to make a quick, yet tall privacy hedge that will be full all year. We planted some Thuja Green Giants. Do you think this was a good choice? If not, what would you recommend? Amanda, Midfield

A: I like Thuja Green Giant, which is a hybrid-form of Arborvitae, but there are some limitations as a privacy hedge. Because it has a triangular, Christmas tree-like shape, there will always be that v-shaped space between the plants, no matter how close you plant them together. However, if they grow tall enough in 5 years, they could be joined together at that spot and above a fence line. So, it sort of depends on if you need the immediate privacy angle. I've always recommended plants like Texas Wax Myrtle and Elaeagnus for privacy hedges, because they will fill out quicker and they are easier to trim for maintenance purpose.

Q: I'm having my foundation repaired. And I have nearly 20-year old Camellias that are going to have to be displaced. What do I need to help them recover when replanted? Alan, Houston

A: Since we treat Camellias as an acid-loving plant, much like our beloved Azaleas, then it would be to your benefit to get some Azalea Soil for transplanting purposes. The local mulch/soil vendor, Living Earth Technology, makes a specific Azalea Soil for this region. And much like the Azaleas, these Camellias need a raised bed of 10-12 inches made from this material. They sell it in bulk at over 10 locations in Houston. www.livingearth.net They also sell it by the bag. Lastly, I would saturate the soil, immediately after the transplant, with something in a liquid organic fertilizer, to help stimulate new roots. I normally suggest either John's Recipe from Lady Bug Natural, or Medina Hasta Gro Liquid Plant Food.

Q: When can I transplant plants such as Esperanza and Hibiscus? Is now (November) okay, or should I wait until spring? Anthony, Orange

A: I'm glad you asked this question when you did and the way you did. While we do talk about October and November being two of the best landscaping months, normally I'm referring to the use of potted material. And while we also talk about October and November as a great time to transplant bulbs, these two plants are tropical and they are not bulbs, and thus moving them in November would be like a death sentence. We have to make sure they make it through the coming winter. When they do, they start new leaves, and that's when they are better suited for transplanting in this region.

Q: How do I know if my Bougainvillea is dead? (March 2010) I have been able to easily break off twigs and they are obviously brown. However, the main trunk seems to have green inside still. If it doesn't have any leaves, is it worth waiting? Rumana, Richmond

A: As with almost any tropical plant that suffers from freeze damage in the Houston area, as long as there is obvious green in the main trunk, then that plant is still alive. In situations just like this, once you're convinced there will be no more freezing weather, you cut back everything to the green wood. Thus, whether you have leaves right now or not isn't the issue. Then after the prune-back, let Mother Nature do the rest. That green trunk means some roots are still alive.

Q: I have a 5 year old Esperanza (Yellow Bells) that is not blooming this year. Do you have any suggestions? Do you think this had anything to do with the January 2010 freeze?

A: I think it had a lot to do with the January 2010 freeze. Much like the Hibiscus, the Esperanza (Tecoma stans) froze back to the ground, but still grew back from the roots. And much like the Hibiscus it takes as much as 6 months to get back to blooming wood, once new growth did come back. What I usually recommend for people in this situation is to start feeding it with a Hibiscus food, especially a water-soluble kind, so we can kick it into blooming gear. Also, on Esperenza specifically, look to see if there are any seed pods on there, and snip them all off. For some odd reason seed pods deter the bloom cycle on these particular plants.

Q: I live way east of Houston, and my large Sago Palms were badly hit by the winter freezes. They are brown and dead about three quarters from the top down. What do I do for them? Cut the top brown out or cut all the fronds off? Marilyn, Sour Lake

A: Like most of the palms following the hard freeze of January 2010, it is a "wait-and-see" attitude we have to take. The fact that you have some green in the fronds is a promising sign. But you simple must wait for any new growth to come out and lay down before you prune all the brown fronds off. This is the rule for almost all palms (Sagos aren't technically a palm, but we still treat them as such). If you prune all the brown off, and since palms (and especially cycads, like Sagos) are such "slow" growers, all the energy of the plant is going into the new growth. And while that sounds like a good thing, on palms it is a bad thing. The new growth will come out twisted and distorted, because it needs "slow-growing" energy. By leaving the brown fronds on as long as you can, you are helping to divert that growth energy.

Chapter 3

Annuals-Perennials-Flowers

Q: What should I do with my Easter Lilies? Should I just cut them down to the ground? Will they come back if I do cut them down? They are in pots if that makes any difference. Nancy, Galveston

A: Now that your Easter Lilies have bloomed and withered, this is that time of the year (April-May) that I get lots of calls and emails about what to do with them. First, you need to know that the Easter Lily will not survive as a houseplant, but it can and should be planted outdoors, where it should bloom again. If its root bound, you will need to score the roots. That kind of "scoring" or cutting of the roots before the actual planting is better for the plant than leaving it root-bound. Water and fertilize with a bulb food, and soon after planting the tops will wither and die, and that's when you can cut anything that is brown back down to the ground. Do not panic, because new shoots will soon emerge that could flower later in the summer. Protect the roots with a thick layer of mulch in the winter, and you should have blooms again next spring. By the way, it is important to note on almost all bulbs, whenever you have browning leaves, just cut them off near the base.

Q: We have Katy Ruellia in our backyard gardens. The plants seem to be spreading across the backyard and into other gardens. What would you suggest we do to stop the spread of these plants? Did we make a mistake by choosing these flowering plants? I love them, and I hate them. What do we do? Mike, Houston

A: That's the conundrum that is Katy Ruellia. They reproduce so rapidly that they can fill in an area in no time, and that's actually a good thing. But because they can propagate by seed so easily, they seemingly pop up everywhere. I too have lots of Katy Ruellia in my landscape, but I simply pull them up when I see a small clump (well before the flowering stage) crop up here and there. You will be impressed with how easy they pull out of the dirt. They also tend to freeze way back in the winter time, and that's another perfect time to get in and harvest out as much as possible, leaving only the established parts to redevelop. If pulling is not an option, you can treat with the typical brush killer herbicides that contain Triclopyr as the active ingredient. You have to add a surfactant though, because much like our weed control discussion, the liquid will roll right off the Katy Ruellia leaves, if there's no surfactant.

Q: I planted Hostas along the driveway, and they receive only 2 hours of sunshine each day, but it is from Noon to 2 p.m. They have burned out. What is good along the house/driveway for replacing these? Can Hostas survive here? Martha, Sugarland

A: Yes, Hostas can survive here, but they need complete shade. They don't handle our freezes very well either and they usually have to be treated as an annual and replaced each and every year. As for replacements, I think a number of ferns would do much better along a driveway, and still deal with the 2 hours of direct sun, much better than Hostas. I'm also a big fan of Coleus and Caladiums, and even the shade-loving versions of these can handle two hours of direct sun better than Hostas.

Q: I want to plant Bluebonnets. Do I plants seeds or plants? When should I plant them and where can I buy the seeds? Phil, Katy

A: October is usually the best month to plant Bluebonnet seeds. Simply put, the wildflowers we enjoy most in the spring have to be germinated in the fall. 20 years ago, that was pretty much the only way you could do bluebonnets, but in the past few years many nurseries and garden centers are carrying bluebonnet transplants, early in the spring, for people that don't want to hassle with the germination process. But to this day, the best place to get wildflower seeds, is based right here in Texas, just outside of Fredricksburg, at a place called Wildseed Farms. www.wildseedfarms.com

Q: We have an Angel's Trumpet plant that is nearly 3-years old and will not produce flowers. Do you have any tips for blooming action? Stephen, Houston

A: Go outside with a baseball bat, and whack the trunk a couple of times. You may think I'm kidding, but there's more science than madness behind the technique. Actually, you need to wrap the trunk with a thin towel, so you don't break the cambium layer in the bark. Then smack the trunk 2-3 times with solid swings of the bat. This will often shock the tree out of the funk that it might be in, and sort of re-stimulate the flow of nutrients inside that cambium layer. It's also important not to prune it at the wrong time of the year. In fact, other than pruning dead or damaged limbs, Angel's Trumpets don't need pruning at all. Lastly, I would consider feeding it Plumeria food or something with a really high middle number for blooming action.

Q: My builder's landscaper installed a shrub he called "bull bine". I can find information about this anywhere. Can you tell me what this is, and even if it is suited for this area. Leanne, Spring

A: You were so close. It's Bulbine, and it goes by other names like Yellow Bulbine or even Tangerine Bulbine. And it is one of the better specimens we can use in our landscapes in Houston. I would have to say that it's still one of my Top 30 small shrub recommendations, as I covered in may last book.

For those who don't know, Bulbine is characterized, by tall spikes of yellow and orange blooms in the spring and summer. It acts like a succulent and yet it is classified as a perennial. But my favorite attribute has to be its drought tolerance once they are established.

Q: I need to know how to make a cutting from my Yesterday, Today and Tomorrow plant. I have two beautiful plants growing by my back door, and I want to take some cuttings. So, how is it done, and is there a best time of the year to do that? Kathy, Houston

A: One of my all time favorite plants, by the way, the Brunfelsia (Yesterday, Today & Tomorrow) is actually quite easy to propagate, and it can be done at almost any time of the year, but May & June may be the best two months. This glorious tri-colored beauty is propagated by what is known as Tip Cuttings, where you take about a 6-inch piece of a stem, including the terminal bud, and make a cut just below a node. Remove the lower leaves that would touch or be below your potting medium. Then you dip the stem in a rooting hormone, dowel a hole in the potting medium with a pencil and place it in there deep enough to support itself.

Chapter 4

Lawn & Turf

Includes:

Synthetic Lawn Fertilization Schedule,

Organic Lawn Fertilization Schedule and

Quick Reference Guide

Q: How do I fertilize freshly laid sod? I've read that I should apply something with lots of potassium. Do you subscribe to that thinking? It was laid at the beginning of February on a new construction. Do you think there's any fertilizer on that new grass anyway? Andrew, Katy

A: Fall Fertilizers (or Winterizers) have long been considered a great "new lawn starter" because of the higher potassium levels – the last number in a fertilizer ratio. So, if you can still find any of those formulas, feel free to use it, but that shouldn't stop you from getting right back on schedule with my fertilization schedule come April 1st. The only caveat I might throw in, is that most newly laid sod actually does have about 30 days worth of fertilizer on it. So, if all else looks normal, you can hold off on the new lawn starter mentality and just get yourself on schedule.

Q: Are there any of the fertilizer services that follow your schedule? I don't believe I've ever heard you recommend a service like that. Why is that? Jay, Houston

A: No, to the first question. You're right on the middle statement and as for "why"; I can only confirm your thinking about "wouldn't it make sense for a well-known fertilization company to follow my schedule?" We've tried endorsing smaller, regional companies, but they either cut corners to save money and "cut" their products in order to save big bucks or change fertilizer ratios for the same reason. I endorsed a fertilization company that did follow my schedule very well, but it sold its list to a big, national company and of course they stopped following the schedule. And in almost every case from my past, we've had to drop them from my endorsement. The national companies are all about "upping" the sales calls or "upping" the visits, attempting to get deeper in your wallets upon every visit. That's their business model, and even if they used the right fertilizers for this area (which they don't) because of that way of thinking, I could never endorse them. But, again, wouldn't you think that if my schedule is as successful as it is for the average homeowner, someone would attempt to follow it on a grander scale? Interestingly enough, while I have had an inquiry or two about attaching my name to such a service, I've never been able to find a company worth trusting to do it correctly – as of today! The reason why, is because they are always trying to find ways to cut corners, cut costs and save money to the bottom line, as opposed to staying true to the schedule.

Q: Do you recommend Palmetto or Raleigh St. Augustine grass for a residential yard? This is for the Baytown area if you think that makes a difference in your recommendation? Gary, Baytown

A: Between those two you really can't go wrong. I think Palmetto has an advantage over Raleigh simply because it is usually a darker green. You might also consider Del Mar or even the newest St. Augustine variety known as Amerishade. Amerishade can develop a shade tolerance over time. The best thing you can do is visit the website www.kingranchturfgrass.com and click on the Turfgrass Selector button. Then click on the zone for your area, and they will recommend over 20 different grasses for that area. You can read the pros and cons of each one and make a truly informed decision on which St. Augustine will work best in your area.

Q: I noticed a tip on a different gardening website for replacing grass sod. It states that the old grass need not be removed before laying the new sod. Is that true? Brandon, Spring

A: First off, what are you doing getting advice from any other website than mine? When it comes to recommendations on replacing St. Augustine, that advice on not removing the old grass, is the worst advice anyone can give. That technique is applicable in northern climates, where fescue or rye or bluegrass might be the grass in question. Those can be scalped to the soil surface and new sod can often be laid on top. In this region, the runners and roots from St. Augustine and even Bermuda are so dense and so hardy that scalping to the soil line is not enough to create a dirt surface where we would want to lay new sod. Here, we Kill-Till-Fill & Sod; a technique where we kill it out with a herbicide, till it all out of there and bring in some new fill dirt where needed. Then we can sod.

Q: My lawn at my bay house was badly damaged by the saltwater from Hurricane Ike. It is mostly St. Augustine. Or I should say it WAS mostly St. Augustine. Can I revive the St. Augustine or should I kill what's left and re-sod? I get a lot of sand in the lawn too. Does that affect what I need to be doing to the soil to get my yard back? Tommy, Galveston

A: There are several things you can and should be doing to a yard ravaged by saltwater. Soil Activators mixed with organic matter, such as compost or humates. Gypsum also helps break down all the salt content in the soil. In some cases, it doesn't matter what the combination is, just get some things down to improve the soil: Gypsum, Soil Activator, Humates, Compost, Seaweed Extract. In your case, while we do need to improve the soil, I usually recommend starting over, because if you kill out everything, and then till in the amendments or new soil as mentioned, a newly laid sod will thrive much better than watching the existing grass struggle to come back.

Q: Randy, my yard was flooded by Hurricane Ike. All my St. Augustine appears to be dead. (December) Just so I would not have to look at an eyesore all winter, I planted rye grass and it's doing well. My question is, will this help my St. Augustine return in the spring, or did I screw up by putting it in? James, Jamaica Beach

A: You didn't mess up at all. In fact, you made a wise decision by sowing the rye grass seed to give you something aesthetically pleasing and that will help with erosion control. However, the rye grass will have zero impact on bringing a St. Augustine yard back from death. There is nothing I can suggest that will bring dead back to life. Most die-hard GardenLine fans probably already know that I'm not a fan of rye grass on healthy St. Augustine, but this a perfect exception to the rule.

Q: Our dollar weed keeps coming back. Last year you talked about what to put on it, but I couldn't find in your tip sheets where this was. Can you help me? I swear we used what you suggested last year, but it didn't seem to work all that well, and now it's back even worse. What did we do wrong? Cheryl, Crosby

A: You probably used the right weed killer, but you likely didn't add the surfactant, which is the most important element when trying to control so many of the broadleaf weeds like dollar weed and clover. That's because the herbicide usually just beads up and rolls right off the leaf surface of the weed you're trying to kill. The surfactant breaks down that surface tension and allows the weed killer to coat the leaf surface, and thus do its job. The other important aspect is to stay true to the pre-emergent part of the fertilization schedule. They will block the weed seeds from germinating if put out at the right times of the year.

Q: What is the best type of grass to sod with in a shady area? And can I do it now (September), or should I wait until spring? Tim, Hockley

A: You probably already know the answer to the second question, based on the advice to a previous question – it really doesn't matter in Houston. As for shade-loving grass, there really is no such thing. There are some varieties of Zoysia and St. Augustine that will deal okay with filtered light, but where there is mostly shade in the yard, we have to think differently by planting ground covers that actually do well in shade.

Q: Is it too late (November) to winterize, if I'm on the organic schedule? Sean, Cypress

A: As many long-time GardenLine listeners know, I have a tenet that says "It's never too late to do the right thing." But I also know that it's not an absolute. The way I approach winterizing/fall fertilizing a yard comes down to soil temperature. If the soil temperature is too cool, it doesn't matter if you're doing the organic or synthetic schedule; it is often a waste of money. What you normally have to ask, is if the night time lows have gotten into the 40s or below, then it's likely a waste of time and money. On the other hand, as long as the temperatures are moderate, in this case "It's Never Too Late To Do The Right Thing".

Q: We re-sodded our front lawn last spring. It's doing quite well, thanks to the schedule you've got us on. My question is, will it hurt to use rye grass during the winter months for visual appeal? Someone told me you don't approve of this. Is that true? Mary, Houston

A: That makes me sound so harsh. Here's my simple take on the subject. If you need rye grass for the aesthetics that you mention, then by all means, do it. If your home owner's association mandates, I don't really get a say, but I think that's hogwash. I don't like it, for several reasons. The St. Augustine under rye struggles to come back in the spring, as opposed to those that didn't have rye grass. While you think it may be visually appealing, unless the seed is germinated perfectly, it seldom looks "right." I've coined the analogy: It's the equivalent to a balding man's "comb-over". They think it looks good, but to everyone else it doesn't look so good. Finally, if you do rye grass, you really should have a "reel" (over-the-top) mower, as opposed to a rotary mower that is standard for St. Augustine. Rotary-mowed rye grass looks awful. There are some exceptions to the use, such as erosion control and needing green grass for an event/party. In almost all other cases, I don't think we should be doing rye grass in our typical lawns.

Q: I inadvertently used Nitro Phos 15-5-10, instead of the Nitro Phos 19-4-10 for my mid-summer fertilizer. Have I screwed up? Is there anything I should be doing to counter-act this act? And don't tell me to look at the bag before applying. I'm already kicking myself enough. Marvin, Kingwood

A: Marvin, why didn't you check the bag before you applied it? (You knew I had to say something!?!) Fear not Marvin. You simply need to get out there and water the thunder out of this fertilizer application. Those familiar enough with my Fertilization Schedule known that what Marvin did was apply the early spring, fast-acting 15-5-10, instead of the slow-release 19-4-10 that I recommend for late spring and mid-summer. The only bad thing that could happen is that the fast-acting fertilizers will not get enough water to dissolve properly and will burn some of the grass. But as long as you water vociferously within the next 24 hours, it shouldn't be a problem.

Q: Could you tell me what causes what I would describe as "runners" in my St. Augustine lawn? While mowing the lawn they catch my feet and the lawn mower doesn't cut them. Do you have any ideas on what this is? Do I really need to get out there with hand-clippers and cut them down? John, Houston

A: Try to look at the positive side of this. If you have runners on top of the grass, it usually means you have such a thick, healthy stand of grass that the new growth has nowhere to go but up top. The quickest way to solve the "runners" problem is to have the yard core aerated/aeration so it opens up space for the runners to move down low. And to remove those that are up, simply stand on the end attached to the soil, and yank them right up and out.

Q: I believe I have burned a portion of my lawn with fertilizer. What do I need to do now? Will this ever come back? Pete, Houston

A: Interestingly enough, fertilizer burnt areas often come back greener and stronger than ever, if you give it a helping hand. More times than not, excessive fertilizer burns the grass blades but does not always kill the root system. Thus, a soaking of soil activators or liquid compost or any liquid organic product will help bring it back. The soil activators will break down the excessive salt content of the fertilizer and then allow what fertilizer is sort of left behind to go to work greening up the grass that will inevitably grow back. It's all a matter of how many times you're willing to soak the area with products like soil activator. I suggest at least once a week for two months.

Q: Love your show and all the information, but my question to you is about all these little white mushrooms in my yard. Can you tell me what is going on here? Is this something I should be worried about? Or how can I stop this Mushroom Invasion? Adrienne, SW Houston

Q: I think my lawn is the only one on the block with mushrooms growing in it. I am curious as to why this is? I live in Cypress if that matters? Mark, Cypress

A: You can see I get this kind of question quite frequently. First, I don't want you to worry too much. In fact, pat yourself on the back a little bit. When you see mushrooms/toadstools that are standard to our yards around here, it means there's a high level of organic matter trying to find somewhere to go, so it spews it outward and upward in the form of mushroom spores. This is also known as Saprophytic Fungus, and if there is such thing as a beneficial fungus, this is one. The best way to deal with mushrooms is to pluck them up whenever you see them, especially before their little canopy spreads out. Throw them away and don't attempt to compost them. And while there is no known "control" method to prevent mushrooms from popping up, once you do harvest them out, I suggest dousing the area with a fungicide to suppress the spores that may have fallen from the mushrooms that already came up. This won't suppress the spores that explode from organic matter in the soil. Usually I suggest something like Consan Triple Action 20 or dusting the area with agricultural sulfur.

Q: Randy, I just got Micro Life Brown Patch Fertilizer (5-1-3). How many times do I have to spread it out? Is this something I have to use more than once, like the fungicides you talk about? Mario, Houston

A: As is the case with almost any truly organic fertilizer, you can use it as often as you think you need for the first year. Most are designed to be used 4-5 times a year during the first year. But much like most organic programs, the more biological your soil gets from organic fertilizers and amendments, the less you need to use in coming years. So, for the first year of using this product, I suggest two times spread over 45-60 days, and then two years and more from now (if you're staying 100% organic) you probably only need one application each fall.

Q: What Medina product do you recommend for new sod? Elizabeth, The Woodlands

A: I believe what Elizabeth is referring to is our recommendation to use Soil Activators like Medina on a new sod installation. Soil Activators will help break down the "mud" that grass has been grown and harvested in, allowing the roots to take hold of the dirt below much quicker than watering alone. You can accelerate the microbial charge that turns the clay-like medium into a more friable dirt. You can learn more about the Medina products at www.medinaag.com

Q: My husband and I are buying a house and the yard is AWFUL! It is loaded with weeds and is super hard and compacted and has hardly any grass. Please help! I have the lawn fertilization schedule and plan on implementing it as soon as possible. What should I do first? Should I pull the weeds or lay a weed killer first? How long do I wait after the weed killer to do the 15-5-10? How long after the 15-5-10 do I need to lay down the pre emergent and slow release? Should I aerate and when should I do it? Rachel, Dickinson

A: Following the schedule, which of course is listed in this book as well, is important, but the key thing you wrote to me about is that the yard is compacted, and that means the very first thing you should do, before any of the fertilizers is to have the yard core aerated. Core Aeration is the means by which we poke holes, or have cores of dirt extracted from the turf in order to create pore space, allow for organic matter to move about and allow the root systems of the compacted turf to have room to move. The aeration process is usually followed by some kind of top dressing soil amendment. It could be gypsum, compost, enriched top soil, humates or even bank sand. But the more organically-driven the top dressing (such as compost) the quicker the lawn will become looser and more mellow. Then you follow the schedule to a "T", from whatever point you're at.

Q: When is the right time to aerate the sod? My backyard sod is compacted because we used to play on it all the time. Pat, Katy

A: There's never actually a BAD time to core aerate the yard. There are better times, but core aeration is always a good thing, and even when it's cold or oppressively hot, there is never a bad time to aerate. The best times, if you so choose, are March, April and May and again in October and November.

Q: After winter how do you cut your grass for the first time? I've been told there is a certain way, is that correct? Leonard L, Channelview

A: What Leonard is probably referring to is "scalping" the lawn. While scalping used to be a time-honored tradition in lawn care circles 20-plus years ago, it is not something we automatically do each year anymore. However, after the extremely harsh winter of 2010, scalping is going to be more important than it has been in more than a decade. The theory here is to open up the lawn to more air and sunshine. But it is also important to note that when scalping, you absolutely have to use a bagging system on the lawn mower, because it is imperative to vacuum up as much of the dead grass (from the freeze) as possible. If you have more green grass than dead grass following winter, then you don't have to scalp as intensely as you might think. By the way, scalping is simply the act of lowering the lawn mower cutting deck by a notch or two. It is always safer to lower it one notch, do the cutting, and see if you need to lower it again to get even more of the possible dead thatch out of there.

Q: I have moved from The Woodlands to the Austin area and am still using the fertilization schedule you have - and it has worked so far with one problem. I can't find pre-emergent herbicides here!! Do you know if I should be looking for a different product name? Jill, Leander

A: You may be focused on only one product name and once you move from Houston, it's essential that you re-educate yourself to proper products for different regions. I'm sure there are plenty of pre-emergent herbicides on the market there, just not with the Barricade active ingredient. Other active ingredients that work well as pre-emergent herbicides are Dimension and Pendimethlin.

Q: What is the spray you suggested that lawn services should use on their equipment to keep diseases from spreading? Does this work to help prevent weed seeds from spreading by equipment as well? Craig, Kingwood

A: What you probably heard was a theoretical discussion about using Consan Triple Action 20 (or a number of other contact fungicides) on the underside of mowing equipment. We also talked about using it on the wheels as well. Consan is a great fungicide and bactericide all rolled into one product. I'm not aware of this practice being promoted or used in the industry, but it's not a bad idea to help curtail the spread of fungal diseases such as Brownpatch. However, Consan does not have any effect on weed seeds. In fact, I can't think of anything that can "sprayed" on lawn equipment that would prevent a weed seed from hitching a ride and finding a new home in your lawn.

Q: I have followed your fertilization schedule using Nitro Phos products since we moved to Houston two years ago. I love it and keep recommending it to my friends. I'll be using the Nitro-Phos Total Brown Patch Control soon but I went onto your website to learn more about brown patch and you mentioned different products for preventative controls and curative controls. Where does Nitro-Phos Total Brown Patch Control fall under? Deborah, Houston

A: Oddly enough, the PCNB-based product you mentioned is both a curative and preventive control. The other product from Nitro Phos that you may have heard me mention lately is also a curative and preventative control, is Nitro Phos Eagle. This has the active ingredient known as Myclobutanil. PCNB stands for -**Pentachloronitrobenzene**. Now you know why I always shorten it to PCNB. They both have the 2-in-1 aspect, but they both only last about 1 month. This means, once you start that kind of treatment you have to keep it going once a month until the temperatures get low enough that Brownpatch is no longer growing/spreading. That's usually when our daytime highs are in the 70s or below and when our night time lows are in the 50s and below.

Q: I have spots of dead grass thanks to a chinch bug infestation last year. It's only dead in spots. 80% Green 20% dead in patches. I don't think it's practical to Kill-Till-Fill. What would you recommend I do? Jeff, Spring

A: I agree that killing off the entire yard because one-fourth is dead is not very practical. You can buy pieces of sod, and patch work in replacement pieces. You simply need to excavate the dead grass away and cut out some other grass to create perfectly squared out "holes." That way you can cut the rectangular pieces of new grass to fit the mold. Just make sure the soil is worked up and semi-organic so that as you lay the new sod its roots are making contact with some loose soil as opposed to compacted soil.

Q: Is it too hot to plant new grass? We have a large area in the backyard that we need to re-grade, and then it will require new sod. Yet, I'm afraid to plant it in this heat (Summer of 2010). Would you recommend a different time? Steven, Houston

A: We have a fun rule about laying new sod in the Houston area that goes like this: "I wouldn't do it when it's freezing (or below) and I wouldn't do it when the temperatures are above 100 degrees." What that means is we are blessed with the ability to lay sod about 11 months out of the year in the gulf coast region. As long as you keep it well-watered after installation, it doesn't matter what month it's done. Are there better times of the year? Absolutely! I especially like seeing sod laid in October and November, because the roots will benefit from the warmer soil, and then once established it will bounce back in early spring. Obviously, spring is another good time, because when the grass is growing so fast, you won't see the seams for long.

Q: Is it okay to mix Bermuda seed into a St. Augustine grass lawn? Would the Bermuda eventually take over? Ken, Humble

A: Interesting question, in that most people want to know how to get Bermuda out of a St. Augustine yard in this region. You can over-seed with Bermuda, but the only way it would take over or thrive in the competition with the St. Augustine, is to mow very short. Taller mowed grass shades our Bermuda, while shorter mowed grass (think like a golf course superintendent) will make St. Augustine unhealthy and allow for the Bermuda to spread.

Q: What's your opinion of Buffalograss lawns here in Houston? Or would it do better in a piney woods environment. Ed, Crosby

A: I'm wondering whether you've mixed some messages with your second question. There is a grass better suited for the east Texas piney woods, and it's known as Centipede, a type of carpetgrass that loves an acid-rich environment, which the piney woods provide. As for Buffalograss, I've never been a big fan. I loved the idea of Buffalograss when it first was introduced. It is/was supposed to be low-maintenance, very slow growing and requiring much less water, fertilizers and mowing. But it never really took off in popularity, probably because, while it did meet all those criteria, it looked pathetic. I've referred to it as bermudagrass on Quaaludes. That doesn't mean it hasn't worked for everyone. I know of some people in the western and northern climates of Texas that swear by it. I just don't think it has a chance in our humidity and in our soils.

Q: I purchased the Nitro Phos Super Turf 19-4-10 you recommended, but the directions do not have my spreader listed. I have a Scott's Speedy Green 1000. I looked but could not find a setting. What setting should I use? Ken, Cypress

A: I've written many a tip sheet in my day on KTRH on this topic. We've referred to it in the past as "Spreader Setting Subtleties". The simple rule on fertilizers, for me, applics to all spreaders and all the slow-release 3-1-2/4-1-2 ratio fertilizers I recommend. No matter how many settings the spreader has, you apply the fertilizer at a couple of notches above "half-way" So, if there are 20 settings, you would apply the Nitro Phos at 12 or 13. As for application of other products like insecticides, fungicides and herbicides, the rule is to apply at one-quarter, or a notch above one-quarter. So, on the 20-setting spreader, you would apply at 5-6. On spreaders of 5 or less settings such as hand-held spreaders, these rules don't necessarily apply.

Q: I'm sure you've discussed this before, but I've been unable to listen. Ideally, which should you apply first and how far apart timewise. Pre-Emergent Herbicide or Fertilizer? Or can both go down at the same time? Pete, Pearland

Q: Can pre and post emergent herbicides be safely applied to a St. Augustine lawn on the same day? I need to treat current broadleaf weeds but also want to prevent weeds yet to come. Sherry, Sugarland

A: I certainly get a form of this question a lot, and there are a couple of times in the year, where there seems to be a time frame where two or three products can go down on the same weekend. Some people worry that it's too much at one time. Fear not! You can absolutely put down two or three products on the same day. One catch is that if you have granular and a liquid product to put down, always put the granular stuff down first, followed by anything liquid. If you have to put out all three products on the same day, it shouldn't be a problem. But in answering Pete's question, both the pre-emergent and fertilizer can go down on the same day, and the order simply doesn't matter. If you want to or can put some separation between the applications, more power to you. Again, the order doesn't matter, but I theoretically like the idea of the pre-emergent first, then the fertilizer. But remember Bill Murray as the camp counselor in the movie Meatballs? It just doesn't matter... It just doesn't matter...It just doesn't matter!!!

Q: I suffered from serious chinch bug damage on my St. Augustine grass, and have sprayed per your tip sheet, and

I think they are all gone. Do I need to re-sod the dead grass? Or will it grow back? Audrey, Tomball

A: Some die-hard GardenLine fans, are probably already answering this out loud. You will probably have to re-sod. Chinch bugs actually kill the grass, and nothing we can recommend will bring dead back to life. And my normal advice is that when it's dead, you have to replace it. However, if the dead is in patches or little bits of dead, then depending on the time of the year, there is a possibility that nearby grass can fill in over about 3 months time. Audrey, asked her question in early August, and that makes for a small potential. If it were in September or October, I wouldn't give it much of a chance. When and where you do replace the grass, remove all the dead material to open dirt before you lay any new sod.

Q: I just heard a call where ya'll mentioned something in the water/irrigation that is causing the grass to die. I live in the same area, Pearland, as the caller and I think I'm having the same issue, because I did water a lot recently. Can you explain more about this? Liz, Pearland

A: Liz heard our conversation about too much Chlorine in the water supplies, leading to a problem with Take All Patch. Too much Chlorine kills off the beneficial microbes and beneficial bacterium that normally eats up the bad bacteria that leads to Take All Patch. If you can install a de-chlorinator, that oftentimes solves the problem. But when irrigation systems, that were installed long ago, are incapable of having de-chlorinators added, the problem just keeps getting worse. The simple answer to the question about treating for Take All Patch and for mitigating the chlorine is to top dress the yard with high-end compost like Natures Way Resources (www.natureswayresources.com) Two-Year Old Leaf Mold Compost.

Q: Will Princess Bermuda grass do well in Spring, TX? I have a need for high traffic grass, in case you have any other suggestions. John, Spring.

A: I'm guessing that you read about this variety online? And usually when that happens, the product often sounds too good to be true. Princess 77 may be a perfect example. Dense Growth; High Traffic Ability; Darker Green Color; etc. etc. While it may have the zone recommendation for our area, what it doesn't have is the endorsement of the major turfgrass growers in our region. As an example you can go to www.kingranchturfgrass.com and see for yourself that they don't even grow it. And that says a lot to me. If you are looking for a higher-traffic bermudagrass variety look for Celebration, CT-2 or check out all the different varieties as recommended and grown by local turf farms like King Ranch Turfgrass.

Q: Is there any way of eliminating this wild ryegrass in my St. Augustine lawn? It seems to be multiplying by the day. This is the first year I've ever had this problem. I didn't use pre-emergent herbicides because I thought my lawn was healthy enough to skip that process this year. Did I make a huge mistake? Margaret, Spring

A: You didn't make a huge mistake at all. I too have been eliminating pre-emergent herbicides from my yard, simply because a healthy yard is the best defense against weeds. However, the weed you are probably referring to is known as Poa Annua or wild bluegrass. The pre-emergent herbicides that block grassy weeds are still the best defense against this weed. But when it does come up, just remember that it cannot handle our heat and will dissolve naturally once the high temperatures settle in. Meanwhile, you can spray products like Image or MSMA on them. Let me be the first to warn you however, that MSMA will do damage to St.

Augustine lawns, so you will need to be very specific in your spot treating of Poa Annua. Also, MSMA will likely be removed from the market by the year 2012, so don't get too used to it, if you know what I mean?

Q: I just had a new lawn installed. When is it okay to start your schedule? And are there are other tricks for new lawn installs that you can enlighten me on? Jason, Montgomery

A: The easy answer to this question is: You pick up the schedule after your first couple of mowing. But as you might suspect it's not always that simple. If the grass is semi-healthy and green looking, always keep in mind that there is an ample amount of fertilizer on the grass from the turf farm. So, what I always tell people with this kind of question is to wait at least 45 days before starting the schedule. On the real coincidentally positive side of things, if the grass was installed anywhere from September through December, and if we haven't had a serious cold spell yet, the winterizer treatments we recommend for lawns in general are also known to be super "new lawn starters." Finally, no matter what you hear about pre-emergent herbicides, they are NOT a problem for newly installed St. Augustine lawns. Pre-emergent herbicides block weed seeds from germinating. St. Augustine does not grow by seed.

Q: After winter how do you cut your grass for the first time? I've been told there is a certain way, is that correct? Leonard L, Channelview

A: What Leonard is probably referring to is "scalping" the lawn. While scalping used to be a time-honored tradition in lawn care circles 20-plus years ago, it is not something we automatically do each year anymore. However, after the extremely harsh winter of 2010, scalping is going to be more important than it has been in more than a decade. The theory here is to open up the lawn to more air and sunshine. But it is also important to note that when scalping, you absolutely have to use a bagging system on the lawn mower, because it is imperative to vacuum up as much of the dead grass (from the freeze) as possible. If you have more green grass than dead grass following winter, then you don't have to scalp as intensely as you might think. By the way, scalping is simply the act of lowering the lawn mower cutting deck by a notch or two. It is always safer to lower it one notch, do the cutting, and see if you need to lower it again to get even more of the possible dead thatch out of there.

FERTILIZATION SCHEDULES

SLOW-RELEASE SCHEDULE (Randy's Choice)

The Slow-Release schedule is comprised of four fertilizer applications, three herbicide applications, two fungicide applications and one iron supplementation (optional).

Early February Through Early March - Pre-Emergent Herbicide -- This will help prevent weed seeds from germinating February through April.

End of February-First of March - Apply a fast-acting 15-5-10. (Example: Nitro Phos Imperial) This will give you a quick green up a month before the slow release part.

April - Slow release 3-1-2 ratios (Examples: Nitro Phos Super Turf 19-4-10; Easy Gro Premium 19-5-9; Fertilome Southwest Greenmaker 18-4-6; Southwest Fertilizer Premium Gold 15-5-10.) These recommendations are for the Gulf Coast region that incorporates the Houston area. However, many varieties from Nitro Phos to Fertilome are available in many other counties and other states.

May - Pre-Emergent Herbicide. This will help prevent weed seed from germinating May through August.

July – Slow release 3-1-2 ratios (Examples: same as in April)

End of August - Fungicide Preventative. Use systemic fungicides to prevent Brownpatch. Examples: Turfcide Terrachlor, Nitro Phos PCNP Terrachlor, Safe-T Green, Fertilome Liquid Systemic Fungicide, any Myclobutanil product like Fertilome F-Stop or Green Light Fung-Away, or any Systemic Bayleton.

End of September - Fungicide Preventative. Use systemic fungicides again.

October – Winterizer Formulas of the aforementioned products.

End of October through November – Pre-Emergent Herbicide. This will help prevent weed seed from germinating December and January.

ORGANIC –COMPOST SCHEDULE

Consists of four organic-compost fertilizations, two natural herbicide applications and one natural fungicide application. As I mentioned earlier, organic fertilizations can end up being a little more tedious and costly, simply because most organic fertilizers only cover an average of 1,500 to 2,500 square feet per bag. Most synthetic fertilizers can cover 5,000 to 7,500 square feet.

February/March - Organic compost or formulated organic fertilizers. Examples: Micro Life, Lady Bug Natural, Better Naturally, Arbor Gate Blend, Nature's Guide, Southwest Fertilizer's Earth Essential, Medina Growin' Green Nature - - as well as any high-end compost like Nature's Way.

February – Corn Gluten Meal as Herbicide. This is a natural way of preventing weeds, but is hard to find.

May/June - Organic compost or formulated organic fertilizers.

August/September - Organic compost or formulated organic fertilizers.

August/September – Actinovate or Agricultural Corn Meal as Fungicide. (Different from the store bought kind and different from the corn gluten meal used as pre-emergent herbicide) Even harder to find than Corn Gluten Meal.

October/November - Organic compost or formulated organic fertilizer as a winterizer.

November - Corn Gluten Meal as Herbicide. This is a natural way of preventing weeds, but is hard to find.

Quick Reference Guide:

Basic Fertilization Schedule

(Rip this out and put it in the garage on a refrigerator or any place you can quickly refer to it, knowing what has to go down at what time of the year for quick action.)

February 1st -- Pre-Emergent Herbicides
March 1st -- 15-5-10 Quick Green Up
April 1st -- Slow Release 3-1-2 / 4-1-2 Ratio Fertilizer
May 1st -- Pre Emergent Herbicides
July 1st -- Slow Release 3-1-2 / 4-1-2 Ratio Fertilizer
August -- Brownpatch Control
August -- Possible Iron Supplementation (Totally Optional)
Oct/Nov. -- Pre-Emergent Herbicides
Oct/Nov. – Winterizer/Fall Fertilizer

Chapter 5

Weed Control & Herbicides

A.K.A – Help Me Kill It!!!

Q: I heard a person on your radio show ask if there was something you could kill Bermuda grass with and not hurt your ground cover. I have that same situation with Asian Jasmine. Could you tell me what the name of the product is? Is it safe for Asian Jasmine too? Victor, Friendswood

A: The active ingredients of the products I probably mentioned are Fusilade and Flauzifop. They are somewhat interchangeable and both take out grass and grassy weeds from groundcover beds such as Asian Jasmine, Monkey Grass and Liriope. The reason they are safe for the groundcovers, are that they are botanically-speaking, plants or shrubs and not weeds or grasses. The two most popularly named products on the market are Fertilome's Over The Top and Green Light's Bermudgrass Killer.

Q: Following your tip sheets, I have had a beautiful lawn for years. But this January it looks like Australian Violets have invaded my lawn. What can I use to get rid of them? Did this happen because I missed the pre-emergent herbicide back in November? Terri, Houston

A: The picture that you sent is not any kind of wild violet, which can be a weed of sorts, but it normally doesn't rear its head until May. In January we can get covered up with Henbit, which is the picture you sent. This is simply a broadleaf weed that can be taken care of with any of the broadleaf weed killers we prescribe in our Fertilization Schedule listed earlier. Remember the key to success? Add a surfactant.

Q: I was listening to your discussion about weed killers that you just hook on to the end of a hose. Do you actually prefer those over the kind you mix in a pump-up sprayer? Or is there any real difference? Mary Jean, Waller

A: In a perfect world, the Ready-To-Spray (RTS) would be a much better deal if it weren't for the fact that often times they don't mete out the spray at the right percentage, and thus we get phyto-toxic burns to the yard. On those that are calibrated perfectly, the dosage comes out too strong and in some cases too weak. If it's too strong it will damage grass blades, and if it's too weak you don't get any weed kill at all. That's why my preference is using concentrated forms into a pump-up sprayer, which also makes it easier to add the all-important surfactant I recommend. You also need to add surfactant to a RTS bottle, and that means taking off the spray top, pouring out a tiny bit of the weed killer and adding the surfactant needed.

Q: I need your help with a weed ID. What is it that looks like a miniature Mimosa tree? It is rapidly invading my yard. And what do I do to get rid of it? Rudy, Kingwood

A: If it's early in the spring, the weed could be what we know as Sensitive Weed (Mimosa pudica). If the weed in question is during the summer and early fall, it's usually a weed called Chamberbitter (Phyllanthus urinaria). In either case, they are treated the exact same way. Any broadleaf weed killer with surfactant is the best control method. You only get one shot at these kinds of weeds, which is why the surfactant has to be incorporated into the spray, because both of these weeds will close up their leaves once touched with anything, including your finger.

Q: I have been fighting what I call Dollar Weed for the last few years. Nothing seems to really get rid of it. It just moves to a new location and starts again. I just put down Scott's Weed and Feed in early March. What are your suggestions? It is a San Augustine yard. Ronnie, Humble

A: As many long-time listeners probably guessed, I definitely don't recommend weed and feeds with atrazine. I'm a firm believer that the true key to success in Dollar Weed control is the surfactant. Most all of the broadleaf weed killers that I recommend will take care of Dollar Weed, if you can get them to actually stick to the leaves of the weed you're trying to control. That's where the surfactant can help. It breaks that surface tension, and softens the water in a way that it creates a sheen of weed killer on the weed's surface. We have so much hard water in our region that if you don't add the surfactant, it usually just beads up and rolls right off the lily pad-like leaf of the Dollar Weed. There are professional surfactants sold alongside of the broadleaf weed killers, so just ask for a surfactant, and most nurseries and garden centers will know what you need. You can also add dish soap of the old-fashioned kind. But too much causes too many bubbles, and not enough doesn't give you the surfactant-effect I consider critical. That's one of the main reasons I like the professionally-made surfactants. They usually have the name or derivation of the words Spreader-Sticker on them.

Q: Love your show and info. What can I do to stop the weeds in my flower beds after I apply the mulch or are the weeds in the mulch? I just can't seem to stop the dandelions from covering everything. Delores, Houston

A: This goes to the pre-emergent herbicide discussion too. Most of the pre-emergent herbicides that are listed in our "Fertilization Schedule" are also good for a top dressing on mulch beds to insure as little weeds as possible. Again, the products with Barricade, Dimension and Pendimethlin are good, as well as Surflan. These are active ingredients in product names and not the "marketed" names.

Q: Several weeks ago I heard you mentioned using a liquid Atrazine to help get rid of Bermuda grass from a St. Augustine lawn. Is this still something I can do if I'm still battling Bermuda? And didn't you say you weren't a fan of Atrazine? Do you have any other suggestions? Bruce, Katy

A: You caught me, sort of! I am NOT a fan of the granular versions of Atrazine which are found in Weed and Feed fertilizer formulas. The granular versions move too easily in the soil hurting the roots of nearby trees and shrubs. But I have, for years, recommended the liquid version of Atrazine as a spot treatment in lawns as a means to reduce Bermuda grass. While it doesn't "kill" the Bermuda, it does make it unhealthy and thus allows St. Augustine to take over. You only have to spot treat the Bermuda, and like many of our discussions on weed control, it is important to add a surfactant so that the spray is directed specifically at the blades of Bermuda. You don't want it to "run off" and drip to the ground below. Too much liquid Atrazine in the soil is not a good idea either.

Q: I have a lot of crabgrass in my yard. It's really too much to dig up by hand. Is there anything else I can do to get rid of it? Chris, Brazoria

Q: I think I have lots of Dallisgrass weed in my front yard. Is there something I can use on it without harming what St. Augustine I still have? Teresa, Pearland

A: There is a very specific organic weed killer that works on Crabgrass, Dallisgrass, Goosegrass and other grassy weeds. It's called Garden Weasel AG Crabgrass Control. It may seem pricey, but it really does work. You simply wet the blade of the weed with a surfactant-and-water mix, then apply the dust of the Garden Weasel AG Crabgrass killer to the wetted leaves. Any other liquid weed control, that has

Crabgrass on the label, will kill all the grass in the area. The Garden Weasel AG Crabgrass control will not harm the St. Augustine in the area.

Q: I have a cocklebur problem. We have not been on a regular maintenance schedule, and I'm sure that's not helping, but is there any advice you can offer to help control these things? Annette, Manvel

A: Burrgrass, Grassbur, Burrweeds, Cockelburs, Sandspurs, and you name it; they are one of the most annoying weeds in our yards. And as Annette noted, they tend to take over poorly maintained lawns. They also like yards with mostly sandy soils. But there are some ways to control these buggers. Keep in mind that Grassburs don't like high nitrogen fertilizers, so anything that is like a 21-0-0 or like a 22-2-2, would be a wise choice for fertilizing in spring and summer. Grassburs also hate humate-rich environments. So, by taking the sandy soil to a more humus-rich level, you will also control their spread. Finally, stay true to the fertilization schedule especially the pre-emergent herbicide applications, because those burs are actually weed seeds, and we have to do all we can to make sure they don't germinate again. As an aside: I'm well aware that cockleburs are completely different that the sandburs, but in the gardening advice world I live in, many people use it synonymously with grassburs.

Q: Randy, I heard you talk about broadleaf weed killers that you can just hook on the end of the hose. But I also know how important adding a surfactant is, so how do we do that to the ones already ready to spray? Marjean, Willis

A: Good question in two ways. First, on most of the ones that I talk about from Bonide to GreenLight, the Ready-To-Spray (RTS) versions are convenient in that all you do is hook them on the end of the hose, but they too could benefit from additional surfactants. Since you've already read how important the surfactant is in previous questions, I won't bore you with the repetitive detail. But the reason this is such a good question is that adding a professional surfactant like Bonide's Turbo or Hi Yield's Spreader-Sticker will keep the product from bubbling up, like when you use dish soap. The trick is to undo the nozzle, empty out maybe one ounce of weed killer, then fill back to top about two ounces of surfactant. Tumble it, so it becomes infused throughout the bottle and then get busy.

Q: Love all your info and have benefited from it in my yard, but how do I keep the weeds out of my flower beds? I apply mulch and I still get weeds. Delores, Houston

A: As long as you don't spray the leaves of the flowers or shrubs in these beds, the broadleaf weed killers work fine. Just make sure you take a piece of cardboard (or something like that) that you can use to block the spray from getting on nearby plants. Plus, you can still use the pre-emergent herbicides as well in flower beds. As long as you aren't growing flowers by seeds, the pre-emergent herbicides are a valuable tool in flower beds as well. Just don't use them in vegetable beds.

Q: What chemical/product do you recommend for TOTAL vegetation killing? My purpose is long-term lot clearing. What would you recommend so I don't even have to use a string trimmer or mow for a couple of years? Lazy Lance, Houston

A: Coincidentally, there is a product in the local market called TVC, or Total Vegetation Control. The active ingredient in this and other vegetative control herbicides is known as Imazapyr. There is also a well-known soil sterilizer, also widely available in the market known as Pramitol, with the active ingredient known as Prometon. They both work as a total kill for the area. Prometon will last longer and move further in the soil. But both are very deadly.

Q: We are having trouble with Water Hyacinths. And we live on the water. What can I treat them with? Actually how can I get rid of them altogether? And where can I buy it? Michael, Kingwood

A: When it comes to the invasive, yet often beautiful, water hyacinth, control is more realistic than eradication. These noxious water weeds can double their mass in under a month, and if left unchecked, can choke out all the other desirable plants. Plus, the stagnant water in and around water hyacinth makes a perfect breeding ground for mosquitoes. Mechanical removal is important at first, and then you can spray a product like Weedtrine-D, which is Diquat Dibromide-based, and that is the standard in the industry for aquatic herbicides.

Q: Besides digging them up, how can I get rid of Elephant Ears? Kelly, Houston

A: You have a couple of options. One is to cut them down to the ground level, and then cover the area with a tarp or thick plastic. You anchor the plastic/tarp down so it won't move in heavy winds, and with no water, sunshine, oxygen etc., the plant's root system will decompose on its own. You can also cut off all the big leaves and leave stalks. Then, inject any kind of brush killer herbicide (usually anything with the active ingredient Triclopyr) and it will decompose the plant from the inside. If you do choose to dig up these elephant ear tubers, you have to get as many of these bulb-like structures out of the soil as possible. After a dig out, if you see new growth coming up, you can treat the new leaves with a brush killer herbicide formula.

Q: Is there a product that can stop the suckers of Yaupons from coming up all over my landscape? Meyer, The Woodlands

A: There is a treatment, but I'm not all that sure how effective it is, especially on Yaupons. I know it works on Crape Myrtles, but I've not heard whether it's effective on evergreens. It's a spray bottle called Sucker Stopper. The active ingredient is napthaleneacetate, which is used in the orchard industry as a plant growth regulator. Otherwise, the continual pruning at ground level will send a botanical signal to the plant to stop sending shoots up at that location, over time.

Chapter 6

Mulches, Soils & Amendments

Includes:

Top Ten Reasons to Mulch

Top Ten Mulches

Q: Randy, where can I find the printed word about how much fill dirt you should put over the roots of existing grass? Losie, Cypress

A: Right here Losie! The simple answer is this: ½ to ¾ of a inch of fill dirt, enriched top soil or compost is what is recommended as a top dressing for yards in this region. In some instances, there can be as much as 1-inch, but that's usually where the grass shows a depression. But the main goal should always be to scratch in the dirt, sand or compost into the root system, so as to allow the grass blades to emerge. I wish there was an easier way to do this, and one day soon there will be an easier way to spread compost or top dress that is doled out by a broadcast spreader, but as of this writing it still doesn't exist, and thus compost or dirt still needs to be raked in over the turf. There is a company in Houston called Green Pro www.GreenProTexas.com that has a uniquely designed spreader that works for the finest of composts. But, in general, there is no easy way for the homeowner to do it themselves.

Q: I went to a garden center that you recommend to get mulch you endorse – Black Diamond Mulch. They had two pallets. One was Black Diamond and the other they said was Black Diamond, but it was packaged for a big box store. The manager assured me they were the same thing. Was he telling the truth? Didn't you say there was only one Black Diamond? Verne, Kingwood

A: You may have mixed the messages a tiny bit, Verne. As long as both Black Diamond bags said they were manufactured by Living Earth or Earth's Finest, you can rest assured they were both the Black Diamond I recommend. Living Earth has made a different label for mass merchandisers in the past. What you may have heard me lament was how many different dyed mulches use the word Black or Midnight etc. in their product label, and how that gets misunderstood by the average person when looking for mulches that I sincerely recommend. Always look at the back of the bag and see who manufactured it. If it says Black Diamond and Living Earth is the parent company, you have my permission to use.

Q: With all this new "mulch" I have in my front yard from a stump grinding, may I use this as a mulch, or do I need to wait? If I need to wait, may I keep it covered so it does not blow away? Or may I treat it with a product and use it immediately? Peggy, Baytown

A: Stop Right There! DON'T EVER USE FRESH STUMP GRINDINGS AS A MULCH!! That is, unless you make compost from it. There is so much nitrogen in the fresh sawdust from the stump grinding, it will pull everything it can from the nearby soil to break itself down. That causes necrotic (yellowing) conditions in the area and the plants and flower beds have less vitality. Mix it with some soil, however, and let it rest for 6 months, and then you've got a good compost you can use as a mulch. The one exception to the rule, is if you put down about 6-8 layers of newspaper, and lay the fresh sawdust on top. This will not leach all the nutrients from the soil, and by the time the newspaper breaks down the sawdust will be broken down itself. And if you plan on composting, then cover it until you use it.

Q: I've been in a newly constructed home for almost 4 years and my soil is still so sandy. How can I make my soil more organically rich? I assume this will help the water get down further into the soil too? Danny, South Houston

A: You can aerate, top dress with compost or aerate and top dress with humates. Either way will start you on a more organically-rich soil. And you're right, in that the minute you do either one of those techniques, the more friable the soil, the better the water will penetrate to the roots. Also, following an organic fertilization schedule (both the synthetic and organic fertilization schedule are listed in this book) will also get you an organically-rich soil over time.

Q: Randy, what is Green Sand/greensand? Is it good for Houston? Or is it something wildly expensive? Steven, Katy

A: Greensand is primarily a supplement in our gardening world and is derived from a naturally occurring ocean floor material called glauconite. It is almost pure potassium and usually contains about 3-5% potash/potassium with a bit of iron and magnesium and 20-plus trace elements. Organic gardeners use it for multiple purposes such as loosening clay soil, top dressing potted plants and greening up some yellowing plants. It's not that expensive as a stand-alone element, but compared to something like a synthetic iron to green up a potted plant, it may seem expensive, because it usually comes in somewhat smaller bags. And there is actually a mine of glauconite in the state of Texas.

Q: What is the difference between molasses from a feed store and a nursery? What about corn meal and corn gluten meal too? Tracey, Cypress

A: There isn't any difference in the product, other than in how it's packaged probably. Feed stores, are likely to have dried molasses, corn meal and corn gluten meal is larger quantities and ultimately at cheaper prices than nurseries/garden centers. The real difference you may be asking about is the difference between molasses and corn meal from the grocery store versus what is sold for horticultural purposes. There is a big difference in that. I would never try to eat agricultural grade molasses, and

I would never try to use food-grade molasses in the garden. The agricultural molasses, corn meal and corn gluten meal is processed so differently. As an example, grocery store corn meal is just the starchy inside of the corn kernel and not effective on any plants. Whole ground corn meal has natural disease fighting capabilities.

Q: Can limestone treatment be used effectively in gumbo soils to break down the clay and improve drainage? These beds are already planted with Knockout Roses and other shrubs. Does this mean they have to be pulled up first? Carl, Katy

A: Let me separate the answers to the two questions. In the landscape world of Houston, we recommend dolomitic lime and gypsum to soften soils and ultimately improve drainage. These are both limestone-based products. But just adding it to a really hardpan type soil over time may not create the better drainage you're in need of right now. Without the benefit of seeing your beds as they are, I normally would recommend re-setting all the shrubs by building significantly raised beds with rose soil. And yes, you can add lime to the mix, but keep the dose low if you're rebuilding the beds.

Q: There is a patch in my yard where NOTHING will grow – not even weeds. The neighbor has Running Bamboo and the last owner, I discovered, used a poison to control the growth. Is there something in the soil, from that poison that is keeping things from growing there? It's also hard as a rock. Do you think that is part of the problem too? Lynn, Houston

A: It could be two issues, but let's focus on the possible herbicide burn for the area. Likely they did use something like a Pramitol or Diquat, which will sterilize the soil, in some cases for two or more years. I would first remove up to 2-3 inches of soil, and then even after bringing in some new soil to fill, I would saturate the area every two weeks for several months with something like Medina Soil Activator. This will "break down" the chemical residuals in the soil.

Q: About a year ago we landscaped our pool. Now a year later, one side has done well and the other side has not. Everything looked the same when we planted them. What could cause this? I don't think it's any kind of leak from the pool. What am I missing? Lorene, Katy

A: There is no simple answer to this question, that's going to make you happy. What you may not understand is while you think they were planted the exact same way and the exact same time, there could have been a distinct difference in how much clay soil the new roots hit on each side. I would bet money that if I tried to "move" the trunk of any plant on the weaker side, there would be plenty of movement, because the roots never established in a hardpan, very clay soil. Conversely, if you did the same test on the healthier side, there would be little if any movement, because of a strong root system. So, you can either go back in and re-set all the weaker side plants, and really make a better raised bed for them. Or you can go in and poke holes all over the place and treat with compost sort of like a modified "deep root" feeding that we prescribe for trees. The goal being to get organic matter to the clay and let it break down naturally giving the roots places to move.

Q: What is your opinion on the Mushroom Compost from the mushroom farms in Madisonville, Texas? I purchased several yards and used some over the weekend, and am now seeing problems in the landscape. Is this too hot? Is it the compost that is killing the plant, or is it bringing out the bad spores that you noted when talking about compost and top dressing this past weekend? Jay, Houston

A: I'm not a fan of mushroom compost in general, because it's 1.) Not real compost/unfinished. 2.) Treated with tons of salt, so that nothing grows besides the fungal spore that is the mushroom. And I think anyone that listens to me knows how I feel about too much salt in the soil. I know there are people who swear by it, but I simply cannot recommend it here. In your situation, I would certainly get it away from the fruit trees and immediately treat the soils below with something like Medina Soil Activator to help break down the salt residues. You may be wondering then why they sell such a product as "compost". Personally, I think no one would buy it if they knew what was in it, which is why they added the word compost. That way they can sell it rather than paying a waste disposal fee.

Q: Last month I had an irrigation system put in my yard. What is the best method to fill in the trenches left after the excavating? Do you suggest topsoil, sand, mulch or a combination of those fills? Chuck, Houston

A: Before I tell you what I would use, I can honestly tell you that any of those ideas work except for maybe the mulch. I usually recommend high-end compost these days. However, one of the standard rules that still apply to this situation is to find fill dirt that matches the dirt you have already. If it's sandy loam, then get the top soil that is sandy loam. If it is more bank sand, then get some bank sand down. But I like compost because it's going to enrich the soil for a longer period of time.

Q: Love your show and all the information, but my question to you is about all these little white mushrooms in my yard. Can you tell me what is going on here? Is this something I should be worried about? Or how can I stop this Mushroom Invasion? Adrienne, SW Houston

Q: I think my lawn is the only one on the block with mushrooms growing in it. I am curious as to why this is? I live in Cypress if that matters? Mark, Cypress

A: You can see I get this kind of question quite frequently. First, I don't want you to worry too much. In fact, pat yourself on the back a little bit. When you see mushrooms/toadstools that are standard to our yards around here, it means there's a high level of organic matter trying to find somewhere to go, so it spews it outward and upward in the form of mushroom spores. This is also known as Saprophytic Fungus, and if there is such thing as a beneficial fungus, this is one. The best way to deal with mushrooms is to pluck them up whenever you see them, especially before their little canopy spreads out. Throw them away and don't attempt to compost them. And while there is no known "control" method to prevent mushrooms from popping up, once you do harvest them out, I suggest dousing the area with a fungicide to sort of suppress the spores that may have fallen from the mushrooms that already came up. This won't suppress the spores that explode from organic matter in the soil. Usually I suggest something like Consan Triple Action 20 or dusting the area with agricultural sulfur.

Q: I have a very soft yard in certain areas. They seem to be away from the house and on a downward slope, but I sink when I walk or mow. There is no underground septic system that I am aware of to leak, nor do I have a sprinkler system. I was wondering what potential causes and fixes may be? Steve, Pearland

A: There may actually be a few reasons for a soggy yard, the most obvious of which is we can get a lot of rain, and if your soil is healthy enough, deep enough, we can get some seriously soggy soils. If a lawn has never been core-aerated, or if thatch is allowed to build up, this too can lead to soggy turf. However, the more realistic answer is earthworms. Actually it can be many different kinds of worms, but it's also one of those good news/bad news situations. Having a lot of earthworms in the landscape is normally a good thing, but when they get too productive in the lawn it becomes a bad thing, and you do need to do something about it. Any insecticide that has a label for normally bad worms such as Grubs, will work to reduce the earthworm population. Readily available products such as Acephate, Carbaryl (Sevin) and Malathion will work against earthworms. But since earthworms are also know to like slightly alkaline soils; another more beneficial way to reduce their population is to acidify the soil. The most commonly known method is to use Ammonium Sulfate or any standard granular Iron & Soil Acidifier.

Q: How much compost do you recommend for top-dressing a St. Augustine yard? I bought about ½ cubic yard a couple of weeks ago, but it doesn't seem like enough for my 3,000 square foot yard. Is there a general rule? Steve, Spring

A: There is something of a general rule. And you're right that wasn't anywhere close to being enough. The experts say that it takes just under 1-cubic yard to top dress 1,000 square feet, applying it from ¼ to ½ inch in top dress. So, in your case, you would have needed just less than 3 cubic yards. I always round up when calculating for compost or mulch, so I would have suggested 3 full cubic yards. And if there was some left over, you could use it to mulch trees or shrubs as well.

Q: How often can I put out compost as a top dressing? My soil is so bad, that I know I need several treatments. Cale, Tomball

A: When starting from scratch, and if your soil is so compacted, I suggest two applications per year for the first couple of years. Once in the spring and once in the fall should be fine. For those with semi-healthy soil, once a year is a good idea. And for those with really good soil, you can do it once every couple of years. There is such a thing as "too much of a good thing" when it comes to compost top-dressing. That's because if you are too organically rich, the soil can become too spongy and/or hold onto too much moisture.

Q: Can anything be done about the kill spots in my grass where the dog has done his business? Alan, Houston

A: We affectionately refer to that as Canine Pee Disease. Either the pup has high acid levels or high urea levels in their urine, that essentially "burns" the grass. Some people recommend drenching the affected area with something like Medina Soil Activator to break down the high level of urea or acid. Consequently, when that is done, the grass often comes back greener than ever because of the urea and/or acid which are natural forms of fertilizer anyway. But what you might also consider doing is "flushing" the dog's system. You'll notice that this is mostly affecting indoor dogs. They hold their pee for so long, that's when the acid and/or urea build up. Keep them outside, if at all possible, for the day, every day for a week. Leave them plenty of water and that will help change the build-up. If you don't have the ability to leave the dog outside for a day, you can also check with your veterinarian about changing the animal's diet.

Q: Several months ago you spoke of digging a trench around the foundation of the home and filling it with rock. I believe it was two feet wide, but I didn't hear how deep or what kind of rock you used. And did you use a different type rock at the bottom versus the top? Andy, Jersey Village

A: You may have misunderstood a little bit about the use of landscape rock. Yes, we recommend landscape rock as a barrier between the landscape beds and the foundation. And yes, it's about two feet wide, but we don't dig a trench in which to put these. What we have recommended for years is to install a root block fabric as the base which you lay the landscape rock on top of. The depth need not be more than 3-4 inches. We usually recommend what is referred to as Bull Rock or River Rock. These two terms are interchangeable and they are the rounded, semi-polished stones that are dredged or scooped from river or creek beds. Bull Rock is usually the bigger of the two ranging from 2-4 inches in size, and River Rock is ¾ inch to 2 inches in size. We do this technique to keep a path between the landscape and foundation, which protects weep holes from insects and allows you to inspect and examine the foundation constantly.

Q: I have a small pile of sand and pea gravel I dug up from under a brick patio that the previous owners of the house had put in. Would this material work well as a soil amendment for planting some trees? Or should I just purchase amendments from one of your recommended soil and mulch yards? Anthony, Kingwood

A: I actually like this idea a lot, and it could save you a bit of money to boot. If you use the sand, pea gravel mix along with the existing dirt, I would do it at the rate of 1 part sand/rock mix to 5 parts existing soil. This will keep the soil loose for the next few years while the tree is establishing itself, and yet give you the porosity you desire for proper drainage. If there is one downside to it, it's that there is no serious humus/organic material, and you will have to purposefully add organic food to the soil on a consistent basis.

Q: Is cocoa mulch available in Houston? If so, where can I purchase it? Roy T., Spring

A: Yes, it's available, but before I tell you where, please give me a moment to tell you why you shouldn't buy it in the first place. I'm an animal-lover by nature, and so even though I may not have a dog or cat in my house at this present moment, I don't want anyone I know to use cocoa mulch, because it is so deadly to dogs. Just ask a local veterinarian. Plus, I'm sure you've heard the advice all these years that dogs shouldn't eat chocolate. Well, this is why you should never use cocoa mulch in my opinion. It's toxic to dogs! And dogs are so easily attracted to it because of the smell. The only caveats to this situation are if you don't have any animals in your own backyard, I could see its use there, and/or if you're convinced that none of your neighbor's have dogs that would be attracted to the product. With all that said, I've seen it at the big box stores more than any other place. In fact, most of the independent nurseries and garden centers that actually have employees that study up on such things won't carry this product.

Q: My dad use to use rice hulls as a fertilizer for his vegetable gardens in the past. I can't seem to find it. Do you know if it's still available and where I can get it? Skip, Spring

A: Technically speaking, rice hulls were never a great "fertilizer" for vegetable and fruit crops, but they were a great way to change soil structures because of the silicates that the hulls were made from. When composted for a long time in this "buried pits" they did become a well-known organic amendment with a bit of compost capability behind it. Unfortunately, that practice of burying the rice hulls in pits has been deemed illegal and so the practice has fallen by the side. Plus, the majority of today's rice crops are now pulverized into a powder to make waste removal more cost-effective, and the powder is worthless to veggie gardeners and fruit growers these days. So, unless you have a way to access the rice hulls from a rice processing facility, it's likely you will never see it again on the retail market for gardeners. Interesting to note though, that the man famous for bringing composted rice hulls to the market (J. D. McMasters), still has a source for them and uses them religiously on his Blackberry crops in Cypress, TX.

Q: Hi Randy! I want your opinion on rubber mulch (recycled tires). Does it harm the soil and/or plants? Sarah, Humble

A: Yes, it does! Just when I thought we were past the serious marketing of rubber mulches in the landscape, another barrage has hit the market. Let's clarify a few things on the subject: 1. Just because you hear advertising for rubber mulches on the radio station I work at, does not mean "you heard it from me" 2. I don't, won't, can't, never have and never will endorse the use of rubber mulches in landscaping/gardens because the leaching of harmful chemicals such as Zinc and Cadmium will poison the soil and the roots. 3. Despite what rubber mulch marketers tell you, shredded hardwood mulches (at the least the ones I recommend) do not attract termites. 4. I understand the need to recycle tires, but why is it every time someone wants to recycle something of toxic origins, they try to figure out how to put it in my garden? 5. **I can recommend** its use for running/walking paths, dog runs and playground material, just not in my garden. 6. You don't just have to believe me; since there are countless documents you can research on line for yourself to confirm the toxicity and dangers of rubber mulches in the landscape.

From my previous book:

Here are The Top Ten Reasons to Mulch, Mulch, Mulch!

1. They are the First Line of Defense Against Weeds

2. They Help Conserve Moisture in the Spring

3. They Prevent the Soil Surface from Caking/Compacting

4. They Conserve Moisture in the Summer

5. They Help Insulate Roots During Drought Stress

6. They Help Insulate Roots During Freezes

7. They Conserve Moisture in the Winter

8. They Break Down into Useable Organic Matter

9. They Enhance the Aesthetics of the Garden

10. They Help Conserve Moisture in the Fall

And Here are My Top Ten Choices of Mulch

(Not really in any particular order, since they all have their good qualities.)

Texas Native Mulch - The name says it all. It's only from trees and debris in Texas and it's usually blended with compost to give it a look that I used to recommend in the past known as Living Mulch, or a blend of Shredded Hardwood Mulch and Compost.

Shredded Hardwood Mulch – There are actually two distinct hardwood mulches on the market. One is shredded fine enough that it is ready to be a compost amendment as well. The other hardwood mulch is more like chunks and pieces of hardwood with very little "shredding". That is why it is imperative to find the hardwood mulches that say

SHREDDED on the label. The benefits of this mulch are many: It stays in place better than most, keeps a rich color longer than others, breaks down quicker into more of a compost and it could be the most cost effective mulch by pricing standards. Some shredded hardwood mulches are known to get an ooze-like foam on the top layer of the mulch. This is simply a saprophytic fungus (a beneficial fungus by definition) and completely harmless to the mulch or neighboring plants. I'll explain more about this fungus later in this chapter.

Shredded Pine Bark Mulch – Much like the aforementioned Shredded Hardwood Mulch, Shredded Pine Bark Mulch can often come in two forms. Obviously, the SHREDDED variety works best for Gulf Coast gardening situations. Pine Bark Nuggets do not fall into this category. While still an attractive, dark style mulch, it does tend to float away easier than shredded hardwood mulches. Its ultimate benefit is for those people with lots of Yah-Yah plants (This is what we refer to in my other books as the plants that like Acidic Soils – Azalea, Gardenia, Camellia etc.Pine bark mulches have a little more acid in them, as they break down in the soil.

Mixed Mulch (A Blend of Shredded Hardwood & Shredded Pine Bark) – THE BEST OF BOTH WORLDS, AND THEN SOME. Mixed Mulches also have the ability, because of the pine bark mulch, to prevent the onset of saprophytic ooze discussed in the shredded hardwood variety. This variety is mostly found in bulk at soil yards and not labeled as such in bags. It can also cost a bit more, even in bulk, than the basic shredded varieties of hardwood and pine bark.

Black Diamond (Another blend of Shredded Hardwood & Shredded Pine Bark – But Darker) -- However, Black

Diamond is a very specifically marketed version of mixed mulch. It comes from the parent company, Living Earth Technology (LETCO), but they make a different signature line of mulches and amendments called Earth's Finest. That's the label that specifically carries the Black Diamond mulch. Some people have correctly noticed that mixed mulches that come from bags, such as Black Diamond, are darker than the bulk version of mixed mulch. This occurs because the bagged material has "composted" a bit more intensely. I've never found a natural mulch that holds its color longer than Black Diamond. Dyed mulches may stay darker longer, but they don't come by it naturally.

Living Mulch (Shredded Hardwood and Compost) – This is relatively new to the Gulf Coast market, but it may be one of the ultimate 2-for-1 bets to come around. Think about it: We need compost to build beds with, and we need our mulches to break down and be part of the beds eventually. I can think of no other way of accelerating the process than by blending the two. Viola! I give you Living Mulch – a perfect blend of compost and shredded hardwood mulches. As of 2005, I am aware of only one company that makes this, and that just happens to be the company that pretty much set the standards for Organic Gardening in Texas -- Garden-Ville. But watch, because 10 years ago very few companies had shredded hardwood mulches in the pipeline. Now everyone has one.

Pine Needles – While pine needles are slow to decompose, the flip side to that is that they are incredibly long lasting. I also think they make an awesome mulch for the Yah-Yah plants because they do impart a tiny bit of acid to the soil for those plants who could benefit from it. In fact, they may be one of the more perfect mulches for tree rings, especially pine trees. Plus, a thick layer of pine needles may be the ultimate weed barrier because you can put it down much thicker than the shredded mulches. As such, I don't know many weeds that try to germinate through such a uniquely intertwined matting of pine needles. Thus, the downside to pine needles is that unless it's for use specifically on some of the Yah-Yah plants or trees, you really don't want to add that much acid over time to plants that need a more neutral environment. Lastly, it's important to note on the downside, that pine needles are not always that readily available in retail settings. However, if you have a lot of pine trees already, you have a free source.

Shredded Red Cedar – Much like the other shredded varieties of wood mulches, shredded red cedar will stay in place longer. The three benefits of shredded red cedar are its color, aroma when first applied and natural insect repellency. The downsides are that it cost much more than any of the other shredded wood versions, it's not the insect repellant panacea that some would have you believe (I'll have to tell you about the story of a fire ant mound that built itself in half of an open bag of my cedar product a few years ago.) and you have to really like or want that red color in your beds. That's obviously a personal aesthetics questions that only you can answer.

Shredded Cypress Mulch – Take much of what we just discussed about shredded red cedar and apply it to shredded cypress mulch. It's more expensive that the average mulch, looks different in color, has a natural insect and reptile repellency and has a uniquely pleasant aroma when first applied.

Compost/Composted Humus -- Let's first assume you have a compost pile. Well, then you can compost all those leaves and grass clippings into a free source of instant mulch. While the upside is that it's free mulch – if you will

– the down side is that weeds love to set up shop in rich, organic compost. To me, there is a sort of a simple irony when developing composted humus. Along the Gulf Coast, if you want to block weeds, you still have to put some kind of barrier mulch on top. Still, by organic gardening standards, composted humus is bona fide mulch.

My Opinion of Dyed Mulch

Many of you may be asking about the advent of dyed mulches. Personally, I would never use them in my garden. I understand they are supposed to "keep their color" for a lot longer than many natural mulches, but they just don't break down into organic matter in the garden fast enough for me. Besides weed suppression, I think the organic breakdown is a true hidden advantage. It's also no secret that when you want to add elements (like seasonal color) to a bed with dyed mulch, all the mulch has to be moved completely aside. By contrast, many of the fine shredded varieties don't have to be pushed aside because they benefit the planting hole. To me, the "color" in the dyed mulches are somewhat phony and not natural looking at all. One day they may perfect this process, to be more like the "shredded" varieties of mulches. Until then, I personally would avoid using dyed mulches.

Chapter 7
Insects & Diseases

Q: My Ficus tree leaves at the end of the branches are rolled up. I have no clue what this is. Do you? It looks like bug damage, but I haven't seen any bugs. Not trying to be "punny", but am I barking up the wrong tree? Vada de Jongh, Alvin

A: It is a bug. It could be one of two bugs. And they are both imperceptible to the naked eye. Leaf Miners, just like those we talk about on Citrus trees are the problem. They tend to leave the squiggly lines embedded in the leaves and the leaves then roll up. The other insect that causes a rolling up on Ficus trees is Black Thrips. If you unroll a ficus leaf with a Black Thrips, you can notice teeny, tiny little bugs that look like a miniscule crazy ant. In both cases the treatment is the same as it is on Citrus. You alternate controls with Spinosad and Neem Oil. Spraying one each week, in alternation, for several weeks in a row. And much like the Leaf Miner, the Black Thrips, while causing the plant to look unsightly are rarely deadly to the plant.

Q: I have something that looks like little yellow seeds all over my Oleanders. Do you think this is a bug? If it is, should I be spraying it? If it's not a bug, can you tell me what it might be? Debbie, Spring

A: It is a bug, Debbie. They are aphids, which love Oleander branches and blooms. If you catch them early enough, you can simply blast them with water every morning for a week as the ultimate "organic" insect control. Frankly, most insecticides on the market work just fine, but they need to be applied at least two times, to help break the egg cycle. Bifenthrin, Permethrin and Lambda Cyhalothrin insecticides all work in this situation.

Q: Help! I got in on the tail-end of your slug and snail conversation. We have been inundated by snails this spring. I've been in Houston since 1966 and have never had a problem like this before. Will you please repeat your comments on what to do? They are everywhere, so can you please help? Louise, Atascocita

A: I've always recommended a two-step approach to slugs and snails. The first step is to treat the area with one of the recommended slug and snail baits we talk about from time to time. One that is organic and works long-term is called Sluggo or even Sluggo Plus. The one that works for me all the time is called Deadline Rain Tough Mini Pellets. This is not organic but works in all situations. Organic controls like Sluggo have to be applied several times. But the second step is using D.E. or Diatomaceous Earth on the soil and around the trunk of any and every plant threatened by the slugs and snails. This tears them up as if they are crawling over shards of glass, but is perfectly safe for humans and pets.

Q: I need a natural solution to get rid of all spiders. I understand that some are good, but I know I have Brown Recluse too. I also have cats indoors, if that makes a difference? What do you recommend? Gerri, Missouri City

A: I sense you were trying to head me off at the path that says "most spiders are good guys, so you really shouldn't be trying to kill them." But I understand people's aversions to crawly things insect and reptilian. So, when you want to control them you've got to control them. Since I can't recommend what I would call typical spider insecticides, I can suggest several of the new "natural" controls that are based in essential mint oils. The smell is good for the house, and the natural mint is a deterrent, and yet if you can actually make contact with the spider the natural oil dissolves the chitin-like exoskeleton of the spider, killing it quite naturally. I don't have any brand names but the essential oils are being sold in more and more garden centers as natural insect controls. You just need the mint-based ones for spiders.

Q: Help me Randy! My Leyland Cypress is loaded with bag worms. The tree is tall too. Is it too late to spray to kill the worms? Is there anything I can prevent this with next year? John, Hempstead

A: You can prevent them next year, by treating with any liquid BT product a month in advance of when you think they normally hit. BT is Bacillus Thuringiensis and beneficial bacterium that targets only the worms and caterpillars. If you can treat with BT when they are eating to create their "bags" then you will never have the problem again. When they are as bad as they are now, you have to remove as many bags as you possibly can and treat again with the BT to snare any other worms that might not have made their next yet. You can also treat systemically with an active ingredient known as Acephate. It's still important to remove as many bags as possible but the Acephate will contact kill what might be left, and work systemically to protect the tree for future outbreaks. Acephate can also be used preventively, if you don't mind spraying a chemical, but this too needs to be about a month in advance of known outbreaks.

Q: Do you recommend pre-emptive spot treatment of chinch bugs? I'm thinking about pre-treating areas of the lawn that do not get as much water as they should and therefore vulnerable. Am I doing a good or bad thing, with this way of thinking? Chris, Magnolia.

A: Before I tell you my answer to your specific question, let's be clear about a long-held tenet of GardenLine when it comes to insecticide spraying. I'm a firm believer in what I call the IPM (Integrated Pest Management) theory, where you don't spray chemicals unless you actually have a problem. With that said, unless you can fix this drainage issue, then I think your theory might actually apply. Just remember, that a healthy, well-watered turf is the best defense against chinch bugs. So, I give you tacit approval, but also recommend you fix the irrigation/soil issue long term.

Q: Help! How do I deal with a growing infestation of Sugar Ants (or are they Crazy Ants)? They are invading the inside of my house. They seem to be smaller versions of what I think are Fire Ants, but they don't bite. I bought an ant bait at the store, which looked like clear syrup. This did not faze them one bit. What can I use that will actually work? Bob, Galveston

A: That sounds like Sugar Ants, and the bait you used was sugar-based, and you need to understand that Sugar Ants (Pharaoh Ants) often times are in search of protein too. There are combination baits at pest control stores and feed stores that have both protein (like peanut butter) and sugar mixed together. In fact, my homemade solution recommends mixing Boric Acid with peanut butter and maple syrup for the dual effect. Dissolve 1 Tablespoon of Boric Acid in the microwave with 1 Tablespoon of syrup. That powder will meld into the syrup and you mix that with 2 Tablespoons of peanut butter. Put it in bait stations around the house, and watch them devour it for two weeks. This is still the best way to conquer Sugar Ants in my opinion, and it's fun to watch.

Q: I have large black ants that are eating into my oak trees and from what I have been told they are resulting in the tree getting what I was told is "Black Heart Disease". What can I use to kill these ants so they don't spread to all my oak trees? Michael, Crosby

A: I'll be honest and tell you that I've never heard of anything known as Black Heart Disease on oaks. But let me be very clear when I tell you that the ants aren't what caused the problem. Carpenter ants such as the ones you described are a symptom of a disease in the tree. What that disease is, I can't tell you without seeing what you're seeing, but the ants are there just enjoying the soft moist wood/bark from the disease. Get a tree professional out to help diagnose the disease, that could be Flux or could be Canker or it could be a number of other problems. In the meantime, you can knock out the ants anytime you want with any spray of any liquid insecticide.

Q: Can you please tell me the name of the organic insecticide that acts like "shards of glass" on the insect as it crawls across it? I also need to ask if it is harmful to small children or pets? Valerie, Jersey Village

A: The product is Diatomaceous Earth – also known simply as D.E. It is perfectly safe for animals and children. But it is deadly to insects, because as they crawl across these Diatoms, it tears up their body. D.E. is a remarkable in that in comes from fossilized water plants, probably thousands, if not millions of years old. But like any powder/dust, you should not breathe it in.

Q: My Ficus tree leaves at the end of the branches are rolled up. I have no clue what this is. Do you? It looks like bug damage, but I haven't seen any bugs. Not trying to be "punny", but am I barking up the wrong tree? Vada de Jongh, Alvin

A: It is a bug. It could be one of two bugs. And they are both imperceptible to the naked eye. Leaf Miners, just like those we talk about on Citrus trees are the problem. They tend to leave the squiggly lines embedded in the leaves and the leaves then roll up. The other insect that causes a rolling up on Ficus trees is Black Thrips. If you unroll a ficus leaf with a Black Thrips, you can notice teeny, tiny little bugs that look like a miniscule crazy ant. In both cases the treatment is the same as it is on Citrus. You alternate controls with Spinosad and Neem Oil. Spraying one each week, in alternation, for several weeks in a row. And much like the Leaf Miner, the Black Thrips, while causing the plant to seem unsightly are rarely deadly to the plant.

Q: I have some kind of bugs on the bark of my Orange tree. They are small like an ant, and gather in bunches. They form like a patch on the tree trunk. Do you have any idea what this is? By the way, when they bunch together they get a sort of gray look to them. Is this something you've seen or heard of? Eva, Wharton

A: I know exactly what those are: Giant Bark Aphids. They're actually kind of cool to watch, but if you wanted to simply blast them with a garden hose, you can do that. Then a day or two later, I would treat the trunk with a typical dormant oil spray so you can take care of any eggs or larvae left behind. If you want an immediate "kill", any insecticide can be sprayed on a trunk of a tree. However, here too, I would come back a day or two later and treat the trunk with dormant oil to kill the eggs. Something else to consider when it comes to bark aphids: if the honeydew is dripping harmlessly to nothing below, entomologists say they are so short-lived, that they will go away on their own.

Q: I've got Aphids on my Rose bushes. I'm really interested in going 100% organic in controlling these pests. Where can I buy parasitic wasps to release into my garden to help my Rose bushes? Are you aware of these as a true organic control? Pat, Houston

A: The simplest and truest organic control of Aphids is a blast of water with a garden hose. Plus, there are countless numbers of "organic" insecticides that will do a number on Aphids, from Rotenone to Pyrethrum to Spinosad to

Garlic Oils. But I've never been a huge proponent of beneficial insects as a control for Aphids. Look at Lady Bugs as a perfect example. Yes, they love to eat Aphids, but they also want to "go west" and that means they don't hang around long enough for long-term control. Parasitic wasps are somewhat cool-looking when you hang their little bag to hatch out. But you have to remember they really only work in greenhouse situations. For outdoor purposes, it's sort of a waste of money, in my opinion. How they work in insect control is that the tiny parasitic wasps lay their eggs inside aphids and the larvae kill the Aphid. They do breed rapidly and the adults fly around searching for more Aphids. But again, this is mainly true in indoor/greenhouse settings.

Q: Last weekend, you talked about using alternating insecticides for control of whiteflies on a crape myrtle. You mentioned Bifenthrin and Permethrin. Can these two be used as alternating control on Hibiscus? Didn't I hear you mention an insecticide you should never use on Hibiscus? Mary, Memorial

A: Yes and Yes! Bifenthrin and Permethrin are safe for Hibiscus. The insecticide I wouldn't use on Hibiscus is Malathion. I talk a lot about the need to "alternate" control products, one per week, alternating week to week for up to 4-5 applications. This helps break the egg-cycle and it doesn't allow the whitefly to build up a tolerance to one particular insecticide. Malathion, by the way, will defoliate Hibiscus, but it won't kill it.

Q: I have a small vegetable and herb garden about 4ft by 16ft and at least 12 inches high. It is surrounded by railroad ties. It gets almost full sun. Would it help to add a mulch layer? Alvin, La Porte

A: I almost couldn't tell where this question was going. I thought it was going to be about the sunlight requirements; which you need at least 6-7 hours of full sun for just such a garden. Then I thought it was going to be about the creosote-treated railroad ties and if they were safe for vegetable gardening; which they are if they are aged, and not nasty with the creosote. Then, the actual question was about mulch. Yes, you should always use mulch or high quality compost as mulch on a vegetable and herb garden in these parts. The more compost-looking the mulch is, the better it will be for vegetable gardens.

Q: How can I get rid of these crazy ants? They are even taking over my hummingbird feeders. Do you treat them the same way you treat fire ants? Laura, Channelview

A: The answer to the second question is usually NO! Crazy ants are the black and much darker ants that don't bite, and can't seem to walk in a straight line. Hence the name, CRAZY ANTS! And while the control products that work on crazy ants will also work on fire ants, the fire ant specific products that are baits/broadcast, don't work on crazy ants. I've always recommended any of the liquid sprays that contain the micro-encapsulated versions of a number of synthetic pyrethroids – Deltamethrin, Cypermethrin and Lambda Cyhalothrin.

Q: Do you know of any insects or diseases that can affect Southern Wax Myrtles? I have a big row on my back fence, and while most are doing fine, there are a few that are slow to grow. Those that are slow seem to grow only on the top and the bottom growth gets lots of brown leaves that drop. Do you have any ideas?

A: It's possible you've heard me say that Texas/Southern Wax Myrtles are fairly impervious to insects and diseases, which is very true. But how they were planted could have a lot to do with stunted growth such as this. While some of the adjacent plants are doing well, it could easily mean that those few that are struggling have really bumped up against some hard, clay soil and the root systems just don't have room to move. To answer the first question: Wax Myrtles, while resilient as any plant, can still get a bit of a fungal pathogen, and a spraying with a fungicide like Kocide (copper-based) or systemic fungicide like Infuse (PCNB or Banner-based) often solves that problem. But where it's obvious to me on the stunted growth angle, I suggest deep root watering/feeding techniques, followed by a more frequent pruning. That's because the more hair cuts you give a Wax Myrtle, the more new growth it will attempt down lower on the plant.

Q: I think grasshoppers, or something, have been eating my Meyer Lemon leaves. Yesterday I noticed that the new leaves were wilted and looked like leafminer damage, but more severe. I cut off the affected branches, but what else can I or should I do? Joan, Houston

A: It could be grasshoppers, since we had a serious infestation in the Houston area in the summer of 2010. But more than likely it is slugs and snails that devour the leaves of many citrus and tropical plant leaves in the summer. You have a couple of options, and the first one is sort of all-encompassing. The insecticide Malathion, which is approved for food crops, will knock out just about any insect on fruit trees. However, if it is slugs or snails, and if you want to be a bit more environmental I usually suggest slug and snail baits at the base of the plant, along with a ring of Diatomaceous Earth (DE). It never works overnight, but over a period of a few weeks, the baits and the DE does a great job of controlling slugs and snails.

Q: We have chinch bugs and live adjacent to a 10-acre lake. What is the best treatment for these critters, without disrupting the wildlife in the lake? Mary Lou, Sealy

A: I'm pleased you're thinking about the environmental impact. However, the normal treatment for chinch bugs is not an environmental threat, unless you purposefully over do it. The best way to treat for chinch bugs is with a liquid insecticide like Bifenthrin or Permethrin, with three treatments in a two week period, thus breaking the egg cycle. To your environmental concern, I would likely agree that a granular application could pose a run-off threat. But the liquid versions of these insecticides don't pose that same problem, unless there was some hideous rain within an hour of the application.

Q: Hi Randy! What type of plant could I plant on or near my front porch, which will keep mosquitoes away? Becky, Crosby

A: There really is no plant/shrub that will repel mosquitoes. There are several plants that have oils, that when released will deter them from entering an area, like Citronella plants and Marigolds. But you have to periodically crush the leaves to release the oils, and then the crushed leaves turn brown, and you constantly have to prune them. However, there is still a lot of research being done on Herbs as natural mosquito repellency. I'm talking about plants like Peppermint, Rosemary, Lemon Balm, Clove, Garlic and Lavender. There are lots of websites dedicated to homemade solutions too for blending many herbs and essential oils that when misted in areas also work as effective deterrents.

Q: Randy, is there a way to kill grubs in a yard and landscape without killing the beneficial worms and all other critters in the soil? Sevin granules say it kills everything, including earthworms. I'm trying to stay organic, so is there anything you can recommend? Roy, Houston

A: You should try Milky Spores. They are a biological control in the bacillus family of bacteria, but they target about 40 different varieties of summer beetles that become grubs. Here's the good news and bad news when using Milky Spores for grub control. Good News: This is the most targeted, organic insecticide you can find, and it really does work, but....Bad News: It can take two years to achieve optimum results, and may seem rather pricey.

Q: Hey Randy, I have this alien-looking caterpillar on my citrus trees. It's doesn't have fuzz or antennas or legs of any kind, and sort of looks like some kind of poop. Can you tell me what this is, and if I need to treat for it, or even if it's a threat to my citrus? Andrew, Galveston

A: You actually did a great job of describing the Orange Dog Caterpillar (why they call it this, is beyond me) but it's actually the caterpillar of what will be a Swallowtail Butterfly. And it mimics a big bird "dropping" so it's not eaten by other birds. This caterpillar will eat some leaves, but is otherwise harmless to the citrus, and becomes a beautiful Swallowtail, so leave it alone. By the way, if you want to see what this critter looks like, or if you want help in identifying crazy-looking insects, such as this, please check out this website. www.whatsthatbug.com

Q: I have a web up and down the trunk of my Live Oak, and it's up on some of the branches too. What is this? Will it kill my tree? Do I need to treat it and if so with what? Al, Friendswood

Q: Randy, I panicked when I went out to get the mail today and saw this creepy web all over my tree in the front yard. What is this, and how did it happen so quickly? Quinn, Missouri City

A: As you can see, I get this question quite a bit. Usually, it's easy to hone in on the correct answer, as long as these webs are not "on the leaves" of said trees. This is simply Bark Lice, a beneficial insect that is actually doing you a favor. They are cleaning up your tree. And as mysteriously as these webs appeared, they will likely disappear just as eerily. The bark louse uses the web to protect itself from being eaten by passing birds. Under that web, while they are still there, they are feverishly working to chew up debris and spores on the bark of the tree. Remember, as long as these webs in question are only on the bark, the critter is Bark Lice and they are a beneficial insect you don't want to kill.

Q: I suffered from serious chinch bug damage on my St. Augustine grass, and have sprayed per your tip sheet, and I think they are all gone. Do I need to re-sod the dead grass? Or will it grow back? Audrey, Tomball

A: Some die-hard GardenLine fans, are probably already answering this out loud. You will probably have to re-sod. Chinch bugs actually kill the grass, and nothing we can recommend will bring dead back to life. And my normal advice is that when it's dead, you have to replace it. However, if the dead is in patches or little bits of dead, then depending on the time of the year, there is a possibility that nearby grass can fill in over about 3 months time. Audrey, asked her question in early August, and that makes for a small potential. If it were in September or October, I wouldn't give it much of a chance. When and where you do replace the grass, remove all the dead material to open dirt before you lay any new sod.

Q: After reading your tip sheets online, I'm convinced that I have Gray Leaf Spot in my backyard. Based on your schedule I am due to fertilize right now. Is this something I should hold off on? I do not want to feed the fungus and make it worse. Please recommend what I should do. Aaron, Katy

A: You are wise to be cautious about this. Gray Leaf Spot is a fungal disease that is exacerbated by high nitrogen-rich fertilizers. So, get the Gray Leaf Spot under control and then after about 2-3 weeks of treatment you should be able to pick back up on the fertilization schedule. There are two readily available treatments for this problem. One is to use a liquid Chlorothalonil fungicide (we used to call it Daconil) at the rate of 4 ounces to 1 gallon of water. The label is not written for Gray Leaf Spot, but we know this dosage works. The organic treatment is a product known as Actinovate, which comes from a Houston-based firm known as Natural Industries. www.naturalindustries.com

Q: My rain barrel has mosquito larvae in it. It is covered with a screen, so I'm not sure how they got in there. What can I put in there so I don't kill the plants I want to water with this source? Barbara, Katy

A: A fun way, but often forgotten, is to add a goldfish or two to the rain barrel. They eat up mosquito larvae the way we devour chocolate. Yes, they sometimes die when forgotten and not fed additionally, but it's a small price to pay. But the simplest way to treat it organically, so you keep using the water for potted plants, is to pour in a microbial larvicide. BT dunks (based in the Bacillus Thuringiensis) have always worked in standing water. The natural bacterium eats up the larvae as well.

Q: We have an ongoing battle with Leaf Cutter Ants. My neighbor and I are trying everything to get rid of them, but none of the regular ant sprays or baits seems to work. Do you have any ideas for control? Janet, Sealy

A: Leaf Cutter Ants are fascinating to me because they will focus on one plant, defoliating it in short order, and then using those leaves to develop their own food source back at the nest.

And Janet is right in one respect, no typical fire ant spray or granule will work on Leaf Cutter Ants. You have to find Carpenter Ant Bait and try to find the home/nest where the bait should go. Specialty pest control companies and feed stores are usually the best place to find specific Leaf Cutter or Carpenter Ant baits. Many sprays that we use for insecticidal purposes will kill the ants that you see, but unless you bait the nest, you will never get full control.

Q: I thought I heard you mention a product to help fight off Southern Pine Bark Beetles and other borers that you simply feed to the tree. It was a ground treatment that you don't have to spray into the tree. This sounds like what I need to save the rest of my trees. What was it? Robert, Blanchard

A: There are actually several products on the market that do this, but the specific active ingredient is what you should be looking for. The active ingredient is Imidacloprid. Some market it under the name Merit, but in all cases it is a liquid concentrate that you mix with water, soak around the root systems of trees, such as Pine trees in this case. The tree(s) take up the chemical through the root system of the tree and keeps the tree protected against most borer-type insects for up to six months. There are other Imidacloprid-based products that are also used an "injections" into the bark of the tree. Obviously the root drench is the easiest and in most cases the most cost-effective way of dealing with tree borer-type insects.

Q: Love you, love your show Randy, but I haven't heard this discussed on radio lately: I have a Magnolia tree in my front yard that is only about 4 months old, and I'm trying to find out what the white spots are on the leaves. What are they and how do I get rid of them? I'm worried that they are spreading to my other plants below. Melissa, Brenham

A: It is a scale insect. And they are actually easy to control in a couple of ways. Unfortunately, there really is no organic way to control these scale-type critters, so you do have to spray the tree with a chemical. The best way to control scale to this day is with Malathion. While it smells bad, it really does do the trick on scale, and on anything that is considered an evergreen plant that might have scale too, such as hollies and hawthorns. But here's a little warning too – to spray in the tree, you really need to be fully clothed and wear goggles and something over your mouth like a surgical mask. That way, nothing gets on your skin, since it can be very irritating. For future reference you can prevent the scale from being a problem on trees like Magnolias by feeding them a systemic Azalea food.

Q: I forgot the name of the product you recommend that will kill spider mites on Italian Cypress trees. Can you please help me with that? Victoria, Humble

A: The systemic insecticide based in Acephate is the normal recommendation, because while it works systemically, which is the important aspect in spider mite control, it also has a contact kill on the outer part of the plant as well. You will be looking for Systemic Insecticides with the active ingredient known as Acephate.

Q: How do I get rid of carpenter bees? Dennis, Baytown

A: The smartest thing to do is treat the area they are working with Sevin dust. But you want to do it when they are not there. For carpenter bees, that quite often is around dusk, when they are out and about looking for pollen. All you do is dust the holes with the Sevin, and when they come back and enter the holes, the Sevin dust will kill them.

Chapter 8

Fruit Trees

Q: I have a Peach tree covered in peaches, but the leaves are covered with tiny little holes. They are small; about the size of BB's being shot through them. Do you know what is causing this and what I can treat it with? Leonard, Spring Branch

A: Sounds like Flea Beetles to me, which are semi-harmless and likely won't affect the fruit. You can spray with almost any organic insecticide or synthetic insecticide to knock down these populations. The fact that they aren't eating holes in the actual peaches is the best news you could hope for.

Q: I bought a bunch of fruit trees (all citrus) from the Arbor Gate, and a lot of them have sprouts coming out near the graft and right where the trunk meets the soil. Should I let them grow? Should I prune them off? Nick, Hockley

A: On citrus, specifically, you should remove any sprout/pup/sport, below the obvious graft. They are best pinched off by hand as soon as you see them, so they don't develop any woody bark. Any growth below the graft is coming from the root-stock plant and probably will never develop edible fruit. This technique does not apply to stone fruit trees, such as peaches and plums.

Q: I purchased a nice-looking 7 gallon Peach tree called a Sam Houston. I thought it sounded like it would be perfect for our area. Checking lists for this area (Deer Park) I'm not seeing them. Did I make a bad purchase? Or is this a new variety that just hasn't made the lists yet? Steve, Deer Park

A: I kind of like the way you're thinking, hoping it just hasn't made the lists. And you would think with the name Sam Houston, it might just be perfect for this area, right? Unfortunately, your first question was more in line with the problem. Sam Houston peaches require about 500 chill hours and because we barely get 300-400, it often never makes fruit here. However, just north of the Houston area,

Montgomery County and above, there are people who can succeed with the Sam Houston Peach.

Q: Can I get Kiwi fruit to grow in the Houston area? Steve, Stafford

A: Probably not! There are some really interesting conundrums in growing Kiwi in this weather. First, while they are freeze hardy, they can't be hit with an early fall freeze or they'll likely never produce fruit. Ironically, most of the standard varieties need 700-1000 chill hours, and as you may have heard, we don't normally get that here. Finally, since they need a 240 day growing period (A tomato is only 70-80 days as a comparison) that usually means it's going to get too hot and humid, for the plant, even if we were to get enough chill hours.

Q: Will mango trees do well here in Houston? I'm really interested in growing one, but don't know if this area is appropriate. Can you enlighten me on the possibility? Rich, Katy

A: Yes, we can grow mangoes, but be aware that they are very freeze-susceptible. Most people that grow mangoes here, grow very specific varieties. And they go out of their way to protect them during cold weather spurts. Essentially anything below 30 degrees can severely damage a mango. Years ago, the varieties of "Julie" and "Manila" were the norm for this area. In recent years varieties from Florida have become easier to grow and more readily available. The two most popular ones are "Carrie" and "Nam Doc Mai." The latter two varieties are usually available at those specialty Extension Fruit Tree Sales, we've talked about before.

Q: What are the chances of growing Pomegranate trees in this area? I grew up in an area of the state where we had them growing all over. Plus, since the juice is so healthy now, why wouldn't I want to grow my own and save money on the expensive juice? Robert, Sweeny

A: Ah, to have been a pomegranate farmer just a few years ago, I could have been a rich man today, considering their popularity and the price people are paying for the product. Yes, we can grow pomegranates in this area, but they likely will never be the size of what you're used to seeing in the stores. I enjoy pomegranates myself, not so much for growing the fruit but for the beautiful, carnation-like flowers they produce in the spring. The variety is the key for this area, and I suggest you stick with area standards: Cloud, Cranberry and Davey. The ones that grew robustly prior to the 1989 freeze were Mae, Eve and Fleishman.

Q: I love your show, and always seem to get my questions answered just by listening, but I have a quick question now. What is the best time to prune Fig trees? Are there any guidelines I should be aware of for pruning Figs? I've never done this before and need help. Wayne, Champions

A: The most important guideline is that they really don't need pruning. Other than keeping the size in check for accessibility purposes, there are no standards to pruning Figs, because they really shouldn't be pruned at all. However, if there are limbs that are dead, or not getting enough sun or rubbing onto other plants or fences, then those are expendable at any time. So, consider Figs self-pruning for the most part.

Q: I heard you mention a new Cherry tree that will actually produce in this area. Is this for real? If so, where can I buy these trees? Don, Clute

A: For years, we never had any success with what would be considered a standard Cherry tree, because we simply don't have enough chill hours, and they require upwards of 1000.

But what you did hear me mention was a combination of two new varieties, Minnie Royal (Can be Minnie Lee too) and Royal Lee. They are smaller, more like shrubs, instead of trees. They have only a 300 chill hour requirement, but you have to have both varieties for pollination purposes. Here's the catch, sort of: They are not readily available on the retail market as of 2010. They are sold almost exclusively at the Extension fruit tree sales that happen in January through February in the Houston area.

Q: On your program this morning, you mentioned a number of soft-skinned Mexican Avocado trees. Your guest said that they are so soft they can be eaten off the tree like a peach. I couldn't write down all the names. Would you mind giving me that list? Also, I'm several miles north of Houston, so does that make a difference? Delores, Plantersville

A: Your location shouldn't make that big a difference, because most of these soft-skinned Mexican avocados have a cold-hardiness to the low 20s. This is another reason why we recommend them so much, besides their creamy texture and instant edibility, as you noted. Here's the list of names to look for: Joey, Opal, Wilma, Fantastic, Pancho and Mexicola.

Q: I have what I believe to be a Mexican Avocado, grown from a seed. I never expected it to do much, but it's already 2 feet tall and I know its root bound in the 1 gallon bucket I started it in. Do you have any transplant suggestions? Is this something I can grow indoors? And probably most importantly, what kind of potting soil should I use? Troy, Stafford

A: It is better that you are propagating a Mexican soft-skinned seed, rather than from a store-bought avocado. Since these are cold hardy, I wouldn't hesitate to get it in a slightly raised bed with Rose soil right away. Even if you want to plant it in a bigger container, (In fact, I would start at 15 gallons minimally) at least start it in Rose Soil.

Q: I recently purchased an Opal Avocado. Do I need to have two avocados for cross-pollination? This is the one of the ones you recommended, isn't it? David, Lake Jackson

A: Opal is one of the many soft-skinned Mexican avocados that work well in this region. But you don't need another tree for pollination purposes. In almost all cases, the Mexican soft-skinned varieties are self-pollinating. Ironically, it's the store-bought avocados, grown from the seed, which need another pollinator in the area, if they ever do get to a productive capacity.

Q: I was told not to plant different Citrus trees too close together, because they will take on the same flavor of the tree next to it. Is there any truth to this? Is there a minimum distance that they should be planted apart in the first place? David, Frisco

A: There is no truth to that myth, when it comes to citrus. However, if you eat a seed of a cross-pollinated citrus, then you'll notice a flavor difference. Let me explain: When a bee takes the pollen from a grapefruit and pollinates a nearby orange, what happens is that the orange flower acting as a female in this case pollinates and this newly formed seed has the "genetic" makeup of the grapefruit and the orange. Now, as the orange forms the flesh that forms around the seed, it is totally maternal or only from the orange tree. So, when the fruit is fully formed the orange flesh will always have the same flavor as the tree it is from. However, the seed has half the genetic makeup of the grapefruit. This, by the way is one of the reasons you can't plant an orange seed and expect it to produce a fruit like its parent tree.

Q: The pecans I have on my Pecan tree are falling. I just moved into this house, and have never had a Pecan tree before. So, is this normal? Is this due to a lack of irrigation, since the house was vacant for nearly a year? Greg, Waller

A: There are numerous causes of premature pecan drop. Some varieties such as 'Desirable' shed naturally. Poor pollination results in a drop from June through July. Planting several varieties helps reduce the poor pollination drop problem. A small insect known as the Pecan Nut Casebearer is the cause of pecan shedding at three different periods of the year; mid-May, July and on rare occasions in late August. This drop is easy to identify because there is a small hole in the base of the pecan. Water stress can also result in pecan drop. Ideally pecans should be watered every two weeks. Three weeks without water is the maximum. Nutritional problems from shallow soil or poor fertilization can cause pecans to shed throughout the year. Water stress in later July and early August is the most common form of pecan drop. As the nuts move from size development into kernel formation the pecan sheds very easily. Any stress received by the tree at this stage can result in major fruit drop. Some trees can lose up to one half of its crop if not properly managed during water stage. My guess is that the neglect from a deep root watering perspective is the ultimate culprit here. Just so you know, watering grass is not enough for watering trees – get this tree on some kind of deep root watering/feeding program.

Q: My Pecan tree did not produce any pods this year. It's about 20 years old, but has always had production of some kind. One year might be good and one year might be bad, but even in the bad years there were pecans. What gives? Am I about to lose this tree? Richard, Sealy

A: As you sort of noted, Pecans tend to produce on alternate years or what is known as a "cyclical" basis. The better the management program the less the alternate bearing characteristic. So, my question to folks like you is "What did you do different in care practices, in the last two years?" If you chose not to stay consistent with a feeding/care schedule, the "off" year could be even worse than ever before. Plus, with the goofy weather we have endured from Hurricane Ike in 2008 to the devastating freeze in 2010, the tree may be out of the cycle it has been on for 20 years.

Q: I know that squirrels are supposed to like the nuts from Pecan trees, but the squirrels in my yard are eating the tree. They aren't eating the nuts. They are eating the bark of the limbs. What can I do? Or do I even need to do anything? Sheryl, Atascocita

A: I have an excellent recipe for squirrel stew, and there is no legal season for squirrels in Texas. Uh, wait… that didn't answer the questions did it? There are a couple of reasons the squirrel is eating at the bark. First, since this is November, they are picking up anything and everything to line their nests for the winter. But more often than not the squirrel-eating-bark phenomenon is not uncommon. It seems that during dry summers/falls, squirrels strip the bark from limbs to get moisture. Try watering the grass at the base of the trees early in the morning (squirrels lick dew off of grass blades). Some people will often leave stainless steel bowls of water at the base of trees too.

Q: Hi Randy! My Blackberry bushes are finished producing (June). When is the best time to prune them back? Also, how often should I cut them back and exactly how far? I'm anxiously awaiting your answer. Steve, Cypress

A: Hold off there, young fella! Don't get too antsy to start cutting back everything just yet. While the summer following the crop is the best time to start pruning there are a couple of basic rules you have to keep in mind. Blackberries are comprised of two types of canes – Primocanes (Some say Prima-Canes) and Floricanes. Blackberry fruit is produced by one-year-old canes (Floricanes). After the one-year-old canes have produced a crop, they decline in vigor or die, and should be removed after all berries have been harvested in May-June. Even as blackberries are ripening this year's crop, it's time to prune them for next year. "Primacanes" –the canes that will be next year's fruiting floricanes –emerged from the ground earlier this spring and in many cases are now five or six feet long. These new canes are readily distinguishable since they have no berries on them and they have larger leaves than the present fruiting canes. The primocanes in erect blackberry varieties are very erect and not branched. Top them now at three to four feet above the ground to force them to branch and develop a hedge shape. Left un-pruned, the primocanes will become somewhat unmanageable. Cutting back the primocanes now will also temporarily remove one of the thorny hazards confronted while trying to harvest this year's crop. One or two more prunings will be needed this summer on vigorously growing blackberry prima-canes. The ideal goal is to have a much-branched, rounded, or box-shaped hedge no more than four and a half feet tall and three feet wide by October.

Q: I have Persimmon trees, but I can't ever seem to get a crop. The fruit always drops before I can get to it. Is it a fungal disease or an insect problem that causes this? Any suggestions you have will be appreciated. Ken, Cleveland

A: It's all about the timing, my friend. First, you also have to know the difference between Astringent and Non-

Astringent Persimmons. Astringent Persimmons aren't ready to eat until they soften on the tree. But that poses a problem because, and this may be your problem, the birds may get to them before you do. However, Astringent Persimmons can be harvested before they are fully soft and ripened in room temperatures, in order to beat the birds. Non-Astringent Persimmons are ready to harvest once they have fully colored. But for best flavor it's still advised to harvest them somewhat hard and allow them to soften slightly before eating. It's all about timing, visiting them regularly and beating the birds.

Q: Randy, when is the best time to prune a Lime tree? And what and when should I feed it? Earl, Bacliff

A: The best time to prune most citrus trees is coming out of winter and going into spring. That ranges from late February through early April for this region. As for the "what" and "when" of feeding citrus, keep in mind, that there are scores of good citrus foods on the market. And each one has different parameters on when and how often. But a general rule for citrus is to feed them every two months starting in March (or right after the pruning) and suspending by end of October. Most of the product lines that I endorse on radio have a citrus food. The three that jump to mind are Nelson's Nutri Star for Citrus and Avocado, Nitro Phos Fruit, Citrus & Pecan Fertilizer and organically, nothing beats Micro Life 6-2-4.

Q: When should I plant the fruit trees I bought at the Urban Harvest sale? I had hoped to have them in the ground. With the latest freeze I am not sure when to plant now. Jeff, Houston

A: Like Jeff, many people buy several fruit and citrus trees at the Extension/Master Gardener/Urban Harvest Fruit Tree Sales early in the year, and normally have to wait to plant them until the weather is just right. That's because, if you purchase a citrus or avocado, and plant them immediately and we still get freezing weather in February through March, it's a death sentence for these young, tender trees. Theoretically, you can plant them immediately, if you're willing to protect them on any freezing night. But the common practice is to keep them safe from freezing weather before you plant them in mid to late March.

Q: Randy, you mentioned the name of the citrus tree you called a lemonade tree variety. Could you mention the variety again please? Pam, Garden Oaks

A: Ujukitsu! This is one of those citrus that are easy to grow, incredibly productive and is that smooth combination of Lemon & Orange, much like a Meyer Lemon. The only real catch here is that it is not as readily available as a Meyer Lemon. But it's almost always available early each year at those Extension/Master Gardener Fruit Tree Sales.

Q: One time you said either a Meyer Lemon or a Mexican Lime did well in a container. Can you remind me which one that was? Joe, Houston

A: Actually both of them will do well in containers. The Meyer Lemon has the potential to get much bigger than a Mexican Lime, so the bigger the container, the better. You can start with at least a 15 gallon container, but many containerized fruit trees will have to be bumped up to a 30 gallon container 5 years later. The beauty of growing lemons and limes in containers is if they are threatened by a freeze, it makes it easier to move them to a more protected area and/or cover them.

Q: I planted a Mexican Lime tree about two years ago. It produced a few limes right away, but over the last year it has not grown at all and never gave me any more limes.

Someone told me it was planted wrong and getting too much water. Is that really possible? Well, I dug it up and replanted it using potting soil and plant food. It's green, but it still hasn't grown. What should I do? I was really looking forward to having my own limes. Dianne, Houston

A: First rule on growing citrus fruit is to remove all the fruit from a newly purchased tree. Let it focus on growing leaves and limbs the first year or two. So, that was sort of strike one against you. Strike two would probably be the wet roots, because yes, too much water is a bad thing for almost any plant, unless it was designed for bog gardening. Your third strike comes when you used potting soil. Most all of our fruit trees, be they citrus or stone fruit, need a slightly raised bed planted with Rose Soil (or a good landscaper-type soil). You should never use anything akin to potting soil for fruit trees. Now, while you think you struck out, at least the plant is still green and if you'll do the slightly raised bed with Rose Soil and feed it nothing but organic food from this day forward, we may actually get limes in under a year.

Q: My citrus trees are in full bloom, but they are dropping their leaves. What is this problem? Or is it even anything I should worry about? Wayne, Bridge City

A: Citrus trees drop their leaves to "environmental changes." That could be the excessive production of blooms, or it could be too much water or it could be a serious fluctuation in temperatures. Don't panic though, because all is not lost. If you can temper whatever the change might be, feed it an organic food like Micro Life 6-2-4, you will likely get new leaves in about a month.

Q: Randy, I have enough pencil eraser-sized fruit on my Meyer lemon to feed a small country. Should I leave them alone or cut some of them off? David, Alvin

A: You should remove some. We call this "thinning" the crop. This applies to stone fruit trees as well, such as peaches and plums as well as others like apples and pears. The idea is to pinch off enough of the fruit when they are marble sized, to leave one every 4 inches or so. You can choose 3 inches, or you could choose 6 inches. It's completely up to you, be the benefit of thinning the crop will allow the remaining fruit to get to maximum size and it won't stress the tree out to have to support an over abundance.

Q: We planted Peach, Apple and Satsuma trees this past summer. The Peach and Apple are loaded with small fruit. Should we remove most of the fruit this first year, or can we leave it all on the tree until its ready to eat? Amelia, Pasadena

A: The gardening rule here is that on citrus, like the Satsuma, you should not allow it to produce fruit for the first two years. The stone-fruit category doesn't have the same rule. However, as we've recommended on the radio show for year, you should do some crop thinning, leaving one fruit about every four to six inches on the peach and the apple.

Q: Randy, I have a Peach tree still in a container that I think really needs to be planted in the yard. Is it too late, (Mid March) since I have 3 peach buds on it? I really want it out of the pot so I don't kill it. Becky, Friendswood

A: You will probably notice some recurring themes throughout this book on answers to questions such as this. As long as it's not too cold or too hot and as long as a tree is containerized it can be planted in the ground at almost any time in this region. Becky's concern is understandable, and it's likely that the buds might get thrown by the tree if it suffers stress, which a transplant can do. But my advice to Becky was to go ahead and remove the three buds, and focus on having the tree develop roots only for the next year, and she will likely have 10 times as many buds next year. Remember this rule applies to stone fruit, but not citrus.

Q: I heard you talking about chill hours for our fruit trees in this area. What are our typical chill hours? Can this help me in choosing the right fruit trees at the local fruit tree sales this coming January? Beverly, Hamshire

A: Needless to say, the colder-than-normal winter of 2010 gave us more chill hours for our fruit trees than we have had in quite some time. But since we normally have limited chill hours it is good to be well-armed with just such information before buying most fruit trees. (Citrus is usually exempt from this chill hour need). There is no simple answer to this, but I'm going to highlight several things regarding chill hours for this question. Chill hours for our stone fruit trees are temperatures between 32 degrees F and 45 degrees F. We need the required chill hours per region to work as a sort of internal anti-freeze for the actual freezing temperatures that may occur. We need fruit trees that average roughly 300-400 chill hours. Usually anything that requires 600 or more should be avoided in this region. There are more and more varieties that require even fewer chill hours, such as peaches and plums that only need 150-200. There has been many a mild winter, where we barely get 200 chill hours. The further you get away from the coast, the higher the chill hour requirement is, and the better chance you can get more chill hours. Use Austin as an example. They have the luxury of doubling the coastal chill hours by getting 400-600 on average. That means there are many other varieties they can grow. Conversely, they need to avoid the lowest chill hour requirements, because once a tree gets its requirement, and if the temperatures are warm enough, it will start growing and producing. The problem there is, if we get a late freeze, and the tree is loaded with blooms, that tree's crop is doomed.

Interestingly enough, when talking about chill hours, if you we get lots of sub 32 degree F temperatures, those negate equally the accumulated hours between the requisite 32-45 degrees F. Use 300 as a base guideline for the Houston area, you go up in increments of 100 or 200 every 100 miles or so. Thus, Montgomery County can grow stone fruit trees that require 400-500 chill hours more often than someone in Fort Bend County. Always avoid anything at 900 in most of what would be considered my listening area. The winter of 2010 was the only time in 25 years we got what would be considered 600-plus chill hours.

Q: Randy, I have a citrus tree I need to re-pot. Can you suggest which type of soil I should use for this? I bought some national brand citrus soil, but am leery to use it now since it actually says not to use it for potting. Any Suggestions? Greg, Houston

A: I have the ultimate suggestion. Nature's Way Resources makes, by the bag, a regionally specific Citrus Soil. This mix creates the best drainage possible, since most people were over-watering them and getting root rot. Check it out online at www.natureswayresrouces.com. It is sold by the bag at many independent garden centers throughout southeast Texas. If you have trouble finding it, good old-fashioned Rose Soil made by Texas-based companies is your next best bet.

Chapter 9

Vegetables (& Some Smaller Fruit)

Q: I have tomato bushes that are about 4-5 ft. tall that had lots of blooms but no tomatoes. What could be wrong? Joe, Richmond

A: Sounds like you didn't get any pollination this year. On tomatoes, pollination happens by hand quite a bit, where some people simply shake the base when it's loaded with blooms so pollen will fall from one flower to another. Wind and insects (not bees on tomatoes) also help, and the manual way is to take a soft little artist brush and go from one flower to the other next time you see a bunch of blooms. I promise a huge difference next year.

Q: How do you prevent or get rid of stink bugs on tomato plants? There are too many to pick off by hand. Do you have any tried-and-true methods? Jo Lynn, Alvin

A: Ah! The $64,000 question! Stink bugs are a true problem for tomato crops in Texas, but it's interesting that there is no singular fool-proof, silver bullet answer. As you noted in the question, many times vegetable experts will tell you that picking them off is the best answer. But what if, like in this situation, that task seems daunting? The trick in controlling stink bugs is using a contact insecticide that is still safe for the vegetable/fruit. I've recommended an organic insecticide for years, known as Rotenone. This is extracted from roots of certain plants, and while perfectly safe for humans/mammals, it has a certain toxicity level on insects.

Q: I think I made a big mistake! I sprayed my bell peppers and tomato plants with Adam's Best instead of a liquid Sevin. I did rinse them off as soon as I realized what I did. Will I lose them? And are the veggies going to be edible? Help me please! Melody, Pasadena

A: I don't think you did anything that bad, because while these products do have a bit of oil in them, they are mostly Pyrethrin-based, and that active ingredient is perfectly safe for the vegetable crops. Again, while you might get a big suffocation on leaves with the oil, this is not going to kill the plant. And it is perfectly safe for the vegetable/fruit in question; just remember to rinse them off very well before eating.

Q: Do you recommend those upside-down tomato planters I've seen on TV? Can you purchase them at nurseries and garden center, or only on TV? Kim, Rosehill

A: I don't normally recommend the ones you see on TV, but I have recommended growing tomatoes upside down. I prefer the method where you make your own from a 5 gallon bucket. But if you choose the kind you see on TV, please use a Rose Soil, blended with a bit of high end compost. And the "as seen on TV" kind is available at Ace Hardware stores as of the writing of this book. There are several websites online dedicated to the 5-gallon bucket technique. As noted in the introduction of this book, this is a great example of doing your own research online; I suggest you use these key words for your search: Growing Tomatoes Upside Down. (As a side-endorsement: Even the husband of the lady who photographed the front and back cover of this book (Julie and Bill Nanni) swears by the 5-gallon bucket technique.)

Q: What can I use to stop worms from eating my tomato plants? Dale, Pasadena

A: You have a couple of choices. Since these are tomatoes and you do want to eat the end product, I would stay as organic as possible and treat the plant with either a powdered version of BT (Bacillus Thuringiensis) or the liquid spray version. BT targets only caterpillars and worms and is 100% organic. There are insecticides such as Malathion, which is approved for food crops, but it has a potent smell that makes it tough to use around vegetable gardens. Another organic method is

Rotenone, which works like a contact insecticide. Lastly, don't forget Sevin Dust, as an alternative.

Q: I planted some cabbage a few weekends ago. I went out to look at them this morning and something had eaten the leaves on a couple of plants. What might that be? What can I do to stop them from eating the rest of the plants? And will the eaten plants grow new leaves? Tammy, Spring

A: In your area, you probably have rabbits or deer. Fortunately, the repellant sprays that are available work on both. Look for something like Bonide Repels All or Liquid Fence type products. If you can get the repellant on quickly, you still have time to grow new leaves. Since the cole-crop (those that we grow successfully in the winter) growing season in the Houston area is quite long – October through February.

Q: I planted tomatoes quite successfully this spring, and while I get nice tomatoes growing on the plants, I never seem to eat as many as the birds do. Do you have any suggestions? Randi, Houston

A: I have a couple of suggestions for you. The easiest one, is to hang something like bright-red, shiny Christmas ornaments on the top of the tomato plants before your first tomatoes start to ripen. Birds that try to peck on those hard, red items will remember that those plants weren't beneficial and they'll find another source. There are also several bird-netting products that can cover the tops of plants and as the birds fly over, they don't see anything red to peck upon. Lastly, I know of several people who use mosquito nets on a permanent basis during the growing season, because not only does it keep birds out, but it keeps several damaging insects and nuisance critters like squirrels away as well.

Q: I want to grow Cilantro in my vegetable garden this year. I have tried several times and it doesn't seem to work.

Am I missing something, or is Cilantro impossible to grow in Houston? Lydia, Houston

A: For the most part, it is hard to grow Cilantro in the Houston area, because of our heat. If you can cheat Mother Nature a bit and get it planted from seed early in the winter, (that also means you have to protect it on nights below 40 degrees) you can enjoy some Cilantro early in the spring. However, the minute we get close to 88 degrees and above as our high temperatures, the Cilantro will begin to crater in our gardens.

Q: We had a raised bed built for vegetable gardening by the builder when we moved into our new home. While they looked good at first, nothing seems to want to grow in them. I guess the soil isn't very good, so what do I need to do to make the soil good for vegetables? Gordon, Jersey Village

A: The best way to start a vegetable garden is with a blend of Rose Soil and Compost. Many people have varying opinions on the ratios, but if you'll start with at least 3 parts Rose Soil to 1 part Compost, this is a good starting point. Keep in mind that some people encourage 2 parts Rose Soil to 1 part Compost. Still others have some Rose Soils, like the ones from Nature's Way Resources, which already have ample amounts of compost in them. There are scores of homemade recipes out there too, where people start with base elements from sand to bone meal to blood meal, to rice hulls to haydite. If you have the time and money to concoct your own soil blend, be my guest. It's just saner and far less work to blend the tow elements of Rose Soil and Compost in my opinion.

Q: What kind of irrigation is best for vegetable gardens? I'm getting all kinds of opinions from drip irrigation to overhead watering to watering by hand. What's your opinion? Dale, Houston

A: If you can devise a drip irrigation system, that's usually the best way to water veggie gardens, because it's only the soil and root systems that need the water. And water that touches the leaves of vegetable plants tends to invite fungal disease, attract insects and cause potential sun scald on the leaves. Watering by hand each day is how the fine-tuned gardeners handle it, but that's specifically for someone who can be out there every day, and the same time each day. In Houston, I would have to say that any kind of overhead system is usually an invitation to such problems. By the way, if you understand that your shadow is more important in vegetable gardening than anything, you can overcome almost any problem from insect to irrigation.

Q: Randy, I tried to grow pumpkins for the grandkids. I planted in September and I barely grew anything before Halloween. What did I do wrong? Frankie, Sealy

A: Pumpkins are one of those crops that take upwards of 120 days to realize a crop. So, it's all about timing. If you want to harvest pumpkins before Halloween, you need to be planting them in late June through July. Planting in September meant you were already 60 days behind schedule.

Q: I tried to grow pumpkins, but all I got were these baby sprouts that fell off. There were plenty of flowers, but so few pumpkins ever tried to develop. I fed them a general purpose vegetable food, and even watered with a solution containing Medina Hasta Gro plant food per your advice. What else can I do next year? Gwen, Houston

Q: I love summer squash and other vegetables like cucumbers, but I can't ever seem to get good production. I get these little squash, but they tend to rot and fall off before they get to a good size. What is going on? Collette, Baytown

A: I put the previous two questions together, because I suspect they have the same problem and that's a pollination problem. When most cucurbit crops such as cucumbers, melons, zucchini, squash and pumpkins drop what looks like prematurely developed fruit, it's almost always related to a lack of or improper pollination. Cucurbit crops need bees to help with the pollination or we have to do it by hand. Where there are absolutely no bees, the hand-pollination method is essential. Then, you must also determine the difference between and male and female blossoms. The simplest way to tell the difference between male and female blossoms on must cucurbit crops is that the female flower has a small swollen embryonic fruit under the base of the flower. The male blossoms are usually longer and without the swollen base behind the flower. Once you know the difference, you harvest the male blossom(s) and open them up to expose the pollen, and rub a little bit of it on as many female blossoms as possible.

Q: My tomatoes are rotting at the bottom of the fruit, right as they begin to ripen. I'm using pesticides regularly, and I haven't noticed any birds. So, what am I doing wrong? Norton, Pasadena

A: You're probably suffering from a common malady on tomatoes known as Blossom End Rot. This is not a bird or an insect problem. It is a sign of a calcium deficiency. You can stop this from happening on the remainder of your tomatoes by adding a calcium citrate product. However, the reason you got the calcium deficiency is probably related to watering extremities. Over-watering after dry periods tends to leach out the calcium. Thus, consistency of moisture and locking in moisture with composts or mulches is essential.

Q: I'm building a raised bed for vegetable gardening purposes and I mixed in some granular weed and feed by

Nitro Phos quite by accident. Will this fertilizer kill the vegetables? Joe, Spring

A: That depends on whether you used the Atrazine or Trimec-based weed and feed. The dark blue bag is Atrazine-based and the aqua blue/green bag is Trimec-based. If you used Atrazine, you will kill almost anything that is planted. If you used Trimec, you can still use vegetable transplants, but you will not be able to grow anything by seed. Trimec works like a pre-emergent herbicide. What I would do, if I were in your shoes, is saturate the bed every couple of weeks with Medina Soil Activator and put off doing a vegetable garden until next season.

Q: I want to get ahead of the Squash Vine Borer this spring. Do you have any advice to prevent these buggers from damaging my zucchini and squash plants this spring? Karen, Friendswood

A: I have a couple of ideas for you. The first idea is to take an empty toilet paper roll or a portion of a paper towel roll and cover it with aluminum foil. You split the roll lengthwise and line the entire thing with foil. Wrap that around the base of the squash-type plant. This will deter the moth that lays the egg in the stem that becomes the Squash Vine Borer. Other organic gardening experts say to cover the transplants with row covers during the critical time that the moth would want to lay the egg as well. Hot Pepper Wax and Neem Oil are also organic sprays you can use to keep the moth at bay. Finally, some people actually take the time to inject liquid B.T. (Bacillus Thuringiensis) into the stems. A worm or caterpillar that bites anything treated with B.T. will die.

Q: I read your tip sheet regarding building raised beds for vegetables and your suggestion for layering with newspaper.

I don't have any newspaper. Can you suggest a substitute or should I just go without it? Jamie, Brazoria

A: Just go buy a Sunday paper this weekend. If you are building a raised bed on top of grass, you really do need to cover the grass with 8-10 layers of newspaper, before building the beds on top. Just invest a couple of dollars on a Sunday for a paper. The only other alternative would be magazine papers, since anything else you buy at a gardening supply store is going to cost you ten times what it would take to pick up a Sunday paper. If you don't cover the existing grass and weeds, you always run the risk that grasses will find their way up from the bottom.

Q: I've been growing tomatoes all my life and I think I've gotten good at it. But the past two years, the plants are wilting after they get about 4 feet high. Usually it happens to them one at a time, right down the row. My soil has always been organic and properly sandy for drainage. I usually add additional compost for fertilizer purposes, and haven't steered away from that course in years. Why are there so many problems in just the past two seasons, when for years, I was so successful? Dale, Magnolia

A: Sounds to me like the soil is tainted. This is why we emphasize the importance of Crop Rotation when growing tomatoes (and many other vegetables as well). You simply cannot keep planting tomatoes in the same place and in essentially the same soil year after year. The devastation of the Dust Bowl, or the Irish Potato Famine can both be linked to one crucial farming mistake: monoculture. Monoculture in farming is the growing of a single crop on the same piece of land season after season. Not only are nutrients depleted, but viruses and fungal pathogens come roaring in to the weakened soil. Even though you think you're adding nutrients or new elements to the soil with the compost or vegetable food, the tomato plants have been draining the soil of many other micro-nutrients and several other beneficial elements. Bottom Line: Never plant tomatoes in the same garden year after year, unless you totally remove the soil and start anew each season.

Chapter 10
Critter Control

Q: We live in Brazoria County. We have several acres and big problem with crawdads (crayfish, mudbugs). The dried mounds seem to dull the blade of the riding mower. I also have dogs in the area so I don't want to put poisons out that might affect them. What can I use? What can I do? Diana, Brazoria

A: Whenever and wherever you have crawdad problems, you have a drainage problem that needs to be fixed. They only like perpetually damp areas. Yes, people have been known to put insecticides in the holes of the crawdad mounds to kill what's in there, but until you solve the drainage problem, this problem will keep popping up in the future. That may mean having someone re-grade the entire area, and it may mean installing things like catch drains and/or French drains. But get a drainage/irrigation expert out and assess the situation first, before you apply anything to the tube/mound. If that seems too expensive of a proposition, then you can use the ant controls like Orthene and Permethrin, because they are safe for animals. Just remember, it will be an on-going battle, until you solve the drainage issue.

Q: Any suggestions on getting rid of rabbits other than trapping or shooting? I have dogs but they are more concerned with napping than chasing rabbits out of my yard. Rob, Houston

A: There are several animal repellants on the market these days, and they do have labels for rabbits. The first one that jumps to mind is a product called Repels All by Bonide. You may have heard me recommend it for deer and squirrels in the past, but it's supposed to work on rabbits as well. It's a unique blend of ingredients that when smelled or tasted causes an irritation in the animal, and they immediately go into a "void mode" where they will get as far away as possible. There is a granular application too, and in some cases using the liquid on plant leaves and the granular on the ground can be the ultimate defense against nuisance animals.

Q: There are feral (wild) cats doing "their business" in my garden and yard. It is a vacation home and not occupied all the time. But the smell is unbearable when we do get down there. What would be the best way to rid the property of cats? Is there any "natural" way of doing this, since we do have dogs and children of our own? Cindy, Bacliff

A: There are actually several natural ways to keep the cats away, and there are some natural ways to deodorize the area, if you will. In no special order here are all the ways I've recommended to keep cats out of your gardens. Orange Oil – mix it with water and mist the soil and mulches in the area, every time you're down there. Cats hate the smell of citrus oil. Chicken Wire – you cut chicken wire to fit over the soil and mulched areas. The minute they dig in what they knew as soft soil and hit that chicken wire, they will bolt and likely never come back. Motion Activated Sprinkler – when a cat or dog enters the area the sprinkler goes off for a minute or two and once again they leave. There are several commercial cat repellants and folks have recommended moth balls for years, but they are all hit-and-miss. But the three ways I describe always work.

Q: Randy, a friend of mine has 3 dogs and her yard stinks! I guess it is probably from all the animal waste. I think it's because there is less sun than mine, and I have 6 dogs and no problems with smell. Is there anything she could spray on her yard to deodorize it. And would it be safe for the dogs? Mary Anne, Wharton

A: There may not be a simple answer to this question, because it could also have a lot to do with their diet or urinary tract infections etc. We mention a product often called Consan Triple Action 20 and it is a great odor neutralizer. I'm also a big fan of a odor neutralizer called X-O, but it's harder to find than Consan. And you're right, that more sun will break down the bad elements of an animal's waste quicker than a shadier environment. But remember, a dog's diet may also have a lot to do with that, and she should visit her veterinarian for help with that.

Q: Randy, we have had a few snakes visiting us in our backyard. Animal control says they are likely Bull Nose Snakes. I realize they aren't poisonous, but I can't handle the snakes, period! How do I keep them away? Is there a spray or granular product that will keep them out? Jamey, Missouri City

A: My wife can't even stand lizards in our backyard, so I know what you're talking about. Keep in mind that almost all snakes like it where they have damp places, plenty of shade and hiding places. So, if you open up your backyard to lots of sunlight, and clean out underbrush, and make sure there aren't damp places, then you've taken the first steps towards control. There are sulfur-based products, which snakes hate, that you can sprinkle in the gardens as a perimeter deterrent. Dr. T's Snake Away is a perfect example. Another smell snakes don't like is Cedar Oil, and Cypress Tree Oil. There are cedar oil products in mulch, granular and liquid that you can spray as a deterrent and Cypress mulch gives off the Cypress Tree Oil. There are a couple of snakes that the smelly-things just don't work on, like Moccasins and Copperheads.

Q: We just purchased some property in Cypress - about 3.5 acres. We have found that it is heavily infested with gophers. We have tried the most obvious - water- even juicy fruit gum (which did kill one). Do you have any suggestions for major removal of these creatures! Debbie, Cypress

A: Many of the more rural properties in and around southeast Texas are infested with Moles and Pocket Gophers for the most part. We don't have the normal gophers that one might think of from the more northern states. But no matter what the critter that digs holes or runs and stays below ground more time than not, the answer to killing them is commonly known as a Gopher Gasser. This is a heavier than air gas that will suffocate the critter in the hole of the run. There are several other chemical controls and poisonous baits, but nothing works as well as a Gopher Gasser. They do go by different names, but any feed store or pest control store will know what you mean when you ask for a Gopher Gasser.

Q: Our Bradford Pears are full of tiny holes, and our neighbor says that it is probably from a woodpecker. What should we do? Will systemic controls like Bayer Advanced take care of this problem? Patty, Houston

A: Patty, you can control woodpecker holes, but not systemically. In fact, the woodpecker in question is affectionately referred to as a Sapsucker. So, using a systemic would actually be detrimental to the bird's health. And we don't like that. The way you control sapsuckers from doing further damage is to wrap the trunk with something we have known for years as Hardware Cloth. What that is to the average person is "screen door material." You can get it off the roll at most hardware stores. Staple it on to the tree, and leave it there for at least 6 months. Hopefully, this will encourage the sapsucker to do his/her damage elsewhere.

Q: This past Saturday morning you mentioned a mouse deterrent. Unfortunately, I did not remember it by the time

I got home. I know it started with a "B". It's supposed to be an odor that the rodents don't like. Can you give me the name of the product? And is it poisonous to dogs? Janet, Crystal Beach

A: The product was Bonide's Mouse Magic. They are little sachet packets filled with mint aromas, which mice cannot stand. It will not work on rats, however. This is specifically for field mice control here in Texas. And unless your dog is into mint smells, it is perfectly safe for Fido.

Chapter 11
Miscellaneous & Fun Stuff

Q: I have a lot of water that drips from my air conditioning unit outside. I was wondering if this is water I can use to water some of my plants? Yvonne, Santa Fe

A: Yes, you can use it for potted plants and vegetable gardens. I even have a colleague of mind that siphons his off to his rainwater capture cistern. Air conditioner condensation water is almost the same as rainwater. They both come from the moisture in the air. In the case of rain, the moisture makes the clouds and then the rain comes down. Air conditioners just speed up that process. And don't believe the myth that air conditioner drip is filled with viruses or bacteria.

Q: My wife and I were wondering what your theme song is? Who did it? Jim, Houston

A: First, you may be wondering why this question is even included in the book. But you might be surprised how many emails I've gotten over the years on this very subject. As of 2010, we are using as an introduction, the song Grazing in the Grass by The Friends of Distinction. I used to use an edited version of Lyle Lovett's Blues Walk, because it had this really nice thing we call a "post" in the radio industry -- this little dramatic pause in the music to introduce myself. Lovett used/uses it as the introductory music to get him on stage years ago. Speaking of years ago, when I worked in the same building with the disc jockeys from a standards music station, several of them joked that I should use Grazing in the Grass as a theme song. After I finally heard it, I was hooked. So, we made that decision in 2010, and have loved it ever since. Coincidentally, we still use the Blues Walk as the closing music for each hour. Those who have been listening long enough may remember the flute-y, pipe organ-sound of the original GardenLine theme song, but I can't remember what it was called or who wrote it.

Q: On "Great Day Houston" You mentioned a product called "VACATION" for plants when someone is going on an extended vacation. Can you tell me more? And can you tell me where can one buy this product? Wayne, Dayton

A: Be careful! While Vacation is a great product and I'll tell you how it works momentarily, I suppose it depends on what you think is an "extended" vacation. While its label says it can help for up to 2 weeks, I say 10 days should be the maximum. Thus, I would never use it for an "extended" vacation. Vacation is an all-natural, anti-drought plant treatment. You mix it with water, drench your plants before you leave town, and no one has to water your plants for 10 days. It causes the plant to go into a state of hibernation for those ten days, and the plant bounces right back to normal, once you start watering again. You should be able to purchase this product at any Ace Hardware store or Nursery or Garden Center that I talk about on my radio show. It cannot be found at big box stores.

Q: What was the name of the product I heard you mention on radio that you use in your moving water feature to keep algae away? Yvonne, Cypress

A: I was talking about Consan Triple Action 20. It is an algaecide, bactericide and fungicide all rolled into one bottle. I would never recommend using Consan where birds like to drink and bathe, but in moving water fountains it does a great job of eliminating a lot of the algae that accumulates. It is a temporary fix, but one that does work.

Q: I'm looking for a leaf rake with nicely padded handles suitable for arthritic hands. Do you know where I might find one? Dana, Missouri City

A: What I have discovered over the years, is that it's not the rake handle that can help with arthritis sufferers, it's the quality of the glove you might be using. The folks at Bionic Gardening Gloves actually had their gloves developed to make gardening chores much easier for arthritis sufferers. If you get a chance look for Bionic Gloves at independent garden centers, but also check them out online at www.bionicgloves.com

Q: I have moved from the Houston area to just outside of Austin. I am still using your schedule, and it has worked great, but I am having trouble finding pre-emergent herbicides here. Should I be looking for a different product or different brand name in this region? Jill, Leander

A: You should be able to find some product lines like Fertilome and GreenLight that are also sold in Austin, whereas Nitro Phos is more available the closer you get to the coast. So, first go back to some independent nurseries and garden centers and ask for Fertilome and GreenLight pre-emergent herbicides as well. Also, Scotts has a good pre-emergent known as Halts. It is normally included in a fertilizer that supposedly controls crabgrass, but they do sell Halts all by itself at some of the bigger mass merchandisers.

Chapter 12

Month-by-Month Gardening Checklist

Gardening Checklist
Month-by-Month

This is one of the few things I've kept from my previous book. Since I got so many positive comments over the years on this checklist, I thought it was worth attaching to the new book as well.

As we said in the past, there are many jokes about why people don't give out information because you might be on a "Need to Know" basis. And when I wrote this part of the book, my mindset is always, What Do You Need to Know going into each month. The beauty of these lists is that you don't need to commit any of it to memory. Rather, just refer to it once a month, so you know what truly has to be done for that month.

I used to tell people when selling my first book, that this is the "best" part of the book, because it was "easy access" information. The idea is, at the first of each month, or even at the end of the previous month, refer to the list to help jog your memory as to what things can and should be done.

So, now that you are the proud owner of this, my third book, *1001 GardenLine Questions*, by yours truly, you are now on a NEED TO KNOW basis. And here's what you need to know on the ensuing pages.

January Checklist

You should plant tulip, hyacinth and crocus bulbs (those that needed refrigeration) all through the month of January. Also, plant any other bulbs that didn't get planted in October & November.

PLANT TREES! (Unless it is really cold) The third Friday in January is often used as a regional Arbor Day. It's okay to plant trees that are containerized in the winter months along the Gulf Coast

Prune established trees in the winter months too. It is easier on the tree to do major pruning during the highest state of dormancy, which is January through February.

Prepare soil/beds for upcoming vegetable gardens later in the spring. It really helps to let the soil mellow for 30-60 days before planting transplants or growing seeds.

Incorporate organic compost to a vegetable bed at 2 to 3 inches per 100 sq. ft.

Check Junipers and other narrow-leaf evergreens for bagworms, spider mites and webworms. Although the plant is dormant, insects can still proliferate.

Extend the life of Poinsettias from Christmas, by keeping the soil moist and keeping them away from drafts and heat. They thrive in temperatures between 60 and 75 degrees.

Feed your cool season annuals, like pansies and cyclamen. A light application of a slow-release blooming plant food like Nelson Color Star will be enough until they need to come out in the spring.

You can start fertilizing established trees and shrubs. You can use balanced synthetic fertilizers on well-established trees (ex: 13-13-13). But you should use organic fertilizers only on newly planted trees (anything less than 2 years old in the landscape.) If you are unfamiliar with the concept of Deep Root Feeding, please refer to the Trees chapter.

Control scale insect on numerous evergreen shrubs like Hollies and Hawthorns. During winter, you can control them organically with Dormant Oil Spray. Malathion is still the best synthetic control for scale throughout the year – even January.

Prune fruit trees. Research information on the internet or in specific books, but the vast majority of fruit trees from stone fruit to citrus fruit require pruning in the winter.

Take in your lawnmower and other power equipment for maintenance or needed repairs. Do it now and avoid the rush that overwhelms lawnmower shops in early spring.

February Checklist

In an effort to avoid grassy weeds like Crabgrass later in the spring, put out pre-emergent herbicides right now. You will also need to apply again in May.

You can prune your Crape Myrtles any time during February. The only "required" pruning is to take off last year's seed pods. Please don't over-prune or prune to the same spot year in and year out. That is what we call the Annual Crape Myrtle Massacre.

If you have broadleaf weeds, spot treat with broadleaf weed killers. Avoid weed & feed fertilizers with atrizine.

You can provide an early green-up with fast-acting 15-5-10s, like Nitro Phos Imperial.. l.

Pinch back or "dead head" the winter annuals like pansies and cyclamen one last time.

Valentines Day is rose pruning time. Prune back hybrid tea and floribunda roses not shorter than 18 inches in height. Make all cuts ½ to ¼ inch above the outward facing buds. DO NOT PRUNE climbing or antique roses, until after their bloom cycle.

Perfect time to prune most of the stone fruit trees like peaches and plums

If temperatures are not too cold, you can try a number of color plants that actually enjoy the cooler temperatures like ageratums, cockscombs, cosmos, nasturtiums and petunias,

Apply Dormant Oil Sprays to scale-prone plants, to help kill any over-wintering insects that might still be around.

Azaleas will lose some leaves in February to make room for March blooms, so don't panic if you see 10-20 percent of the leaves on the ground.

DO NOT PRUNE small trees and shrubs that are likely to have blooms. You will be cutting off blooming wood at this time of the year.

Fertilize Trees and Shrubs if you didn't do anything January. Wait on feeding Azaleas and Camellias until after their blooms season.

Trim up and shape up groundcovers like Asiatic Jasmine. This will help them to spread faster in March and April.

If you have Pecan Trees, start feeding them now.

You can start mowing grass for the first time. I suggest you use a bagger to gather up all the debris and dormant grass for the first two to three mowings each year.

Plant the later-blooming bulbs now, such as Amaryllis, Cannas, Gladiolus etc.

March Checklist

Feed azaleas and camellias, once they are finished blooming. Then, feed them again in six weeks. If lacebugs have been a problem in the past, feed with systemic azalea foods.

Prune azaleas after the bloom season as well. Try not to prune more than one-third.

Fertilize roses once a month from now until the end of September. They are heavy feeders.

Begin a fungicide regimen for hybrid tea and floribunda roses, if they are prone to black spot. This requires either a weekly or bi-weekly application, depending on the fungicide.

Good time to replace mulching materials around trees, shrub beds and flower beds, if you haven't done so in February.

Vegetable gardens should have many of their transplants in ground by now. Don't wait until too far into April. You have to cheat Mother Nature along the Gulf Coast

Bag your grass clippings at least once more before mulch-mowing for the rest of the spring and summer.

Only light pruning should be done on trees, in order to clean up dead or damaged limbs. Remember, major pruning of large limbs is better for the trees in January or February.

If you've got Pecan trees, and didn't feed them in February, do so now.

Be on the lookout for pillbug and sowbug infestations. You can use any bifenthrin or sevin-based insecticide, or look specifically for pillbug/sowbug bait.

You can control the caterpillars/worms that defoliate trees in March/April, by treating all new leaves with a BT (bascillius thuringeinsis) organically-derived control.

Buy your slow-release lawn fertilizers now, and be ready for application in April.

Pinch back/prune back established perennials, even after they set their first sprouts.

April Checklist

If you're following my lawn fertilization schedule from the TURF CARE chapter, this is the time for the first slow-release 3-1-2/4-1-2 ratio. Do not use weed & feed formulas containing Atrizine.

Watch newspapers and other publicity for information regarding wildflower trails, and plan to take a trip to enjoy this beautiful natural resource.

Continue to spray your roses weekly or bi-weekly for control of black spot.

Plant your spring flowers/annuals now. However, when selecting annual transplants/color flats, the shorter, more compact ones. The taller they are, the more root bound they are likely to be.

This is the best month for re-potting overgrown or root-bound house plants/tropicals.

Move your lawn mower to its highest setting for the rest of the year. And start mulch-mowing until October.

Plant a tree for National Arbor Day and/or Earth Day, normally in April.

Good month to start planting grass, now that day time temperatures rising. This is an even better time to germinate Bermuda grass seed.

To help control fleas, use insecticides like Bifenthrin and Triazicide in outdoor locations.

Use Insect Growth Regulators/IGRs inside the house.

Outside tropical flowering plants, like Hibiscus, Alamanda and Bougainvilleas need tropical plant foods like Hibiscus food. Don't use "bloom boosters."

Most all flower and shrub transplants do best in flower beds that have been raised a minimum of 6-8 inches above the soil line. 10-12 inches is even better. Use a Rose Soil in almost all cases.

Although Bluebonnets and other wildflowers look great on the roadsides, they are best planted by seed in October for your own flowerbeds.

It may be too late to transplant tomato plants by the end of April, but you can choose somewhat larger plants to give you a head start.

May Checklist

Put down a Pre-Emergent Herbicide, especially the ones that control grassy weeds. Dimension, Barricade or Pendimethlin for the 2-in-1 pre-emergent; Amaze or Betasan for the grassy-weed-only pre-emergent. This prevents weeds like crabgrass in the summer.

This is the best time to start transplanting the heat loving annuals and perennials like Vincas, Caladiums, Zinnias, Purslane, Moss Rose and Copper Plants.

This is another good month to replace or replenish mulch, especially if you didn't do it from January through April.

Continue to feed your roses a monthly application of rose food, since they are heavy feeders.

Start looking for Powdery Mildew on Crape Myrtles. Fungicides like Kocide, Consan, Mancozeb and any Banner-based fungicide will work. Organically, Neem Oil and Actinovate have shown great results on Powdery Mildew in the past few years.

If you didn't do the April application of the slow-release 3-1-2/4-1-2 fertilizer (per my schedule), do so now. Remember, "It's never too late to do the right thing."

Be on the lookout for fungal leaf spots on many shrubs: Photinias, Ligustrums, Hawthorns, Viburnums etc. Fungal leaf spot can be controlled with most systemic fungicides – Banner-based, Kocide, Mancozeb etc.

Be on the lookout for a myriad of fungal diseases on vegetable crops, especially tomatoes. If you see any sign of fungal disease start and maintain a weekly application of any Daconil-based fungicide (Also known as chlorothalonil).

Nutgrass can be controlled with one of two specific herbicides, Sedgehammer or Image.

Image herbicide can also help control Virginia Buttonweed, but only if the daytime temperatures have not exceeded 90 degrees.

Best way to control aphids on plants like Crape Myrtles and other flowering plants, is to feed them a Systemic Rose Food.

Best month to transplant large specimen oleanders.

Don't forget Mother's Day! Potted plants and color-bowls make great gifts.

June Checklist

Develop good irrigation practices for your turfgrass. As a general rule, most grasses need an inch or more of water per week, until daytime temperatures start getting above 90 degrees. Then it can use that inch of moisture every few days.

The best time to water turfgrass is in the early morning hours. Two times you should never water grass in the summer are 1.) 3-7 p.m; there's too much evaporation because of the heat and wind. 2.) 7 p.m. to Midnight; get out that practice or you will be inviting Brownpatch and other fungal disease with that much moisture on the yard all night.

If you don't already have Hibiscus, this is a great month to plant them, and get instant results. While they love our heat, if you can protect them from the late day sun, they will perform even better.

Be on the lookout for Chinch Bug damage on turf, especially near driveways and sidewalks.

Remember to feed tropical flowering plants like Hibiscus and Bougainvilleas with tropical plant foods, not bloom-booster plant foods with high middle numbers.

Make critical notes of your landscape during these hotter summer months. It helps to understand what needs more water than normal, what is growing too fast and how can the landscaping be altered or rearranged.

Spider mites are serious problems on evergreen conifirs like Juniper and Arborvitaes. You can control them with systemic insecticides like Acephate (used to be Orthene) or Disyston or Kelthane. Newer products with Merit will also work.

Most shredded wood mulches should be applied or re-applied to help retain valuable soil moisture and continue to block weeds.

You can do the summer application of the 3-1-2/4-1-2 controlled release fertilizer per the schedule towards the end of June.

Use of iron/soil acidifier supplements can begin in June. This corrects plants with chlorosis or iron deficiencies, indicated by leaves with green veins but yellow tissue everywhere else.

July Checklist

Roses can be pruned very lightly to keep them productive and vibrant during the hotter summer months.

If you're looking for a new annual that is different in size, shape and color then look for Copper Plants or Copper Leaf Plants. They thrive in the heat of July through September.

How is your watering/irrigation regimen? Remember as the temperatures increase, so should your irrigation schedule.

If you aren't watering/irrigating early in the morning, start doing so now. Night time watering/irrigation invites fungal diseases.

Watch for signs of lacebug damage on Azaleas, indicated by a mottled, washed out leaf. Treat with systemic insecticides like Acephate, Merit or Disyston. Also, do at least one application of a liquid insecticide, like Bifenthrin, on the undersides of the leaves.

If you didn't do your slow-release 3-1-2/4-1-2 ratio fertilizer towards the end of June (per the fertilization schedule in the Turf Chapter) then do so NOW! Avoid weed & feed fertilizers at all costs.

If you're interested in a fall vegetable garden, start preparing the bed now. Refer to chapter on Soils, Amendments and Mulches.

Roses could use that ever-so-light pruning, if you didn't do it in June.

You can try to extend the blooming season of Crape Myrtles by pruning off the expiring bloom heads. This can encourage a new -- albeit somewhat smaller – flush of blooms.

Black Sooty Mold on any evergreen plant, flowering shrub, perennial or tree usually indicates an insect problem. It could be whiteflies, aphids, scale or mealy bugs. Treat for the insect first, then you can wash off the black sooty mold with soapy water or Consan Triple Action 20.

Hold off on any major pruning of larger trees and shrubs. December through March is considered the best time to perform major pruning. Light pruning of hedge row shrubs is acceptable.

August Checklist

This is the last time you can prune off expiring Crape Myrtle seed pod heads to encourage one last blast of blooms into September.

Azalea beds may require more irrigation than normal, because the root systems grow so shallow and want to grow laterally, not necessarily deeply.

Start thinking about building a compost pile. This will accommodate all your fall leaves and grass clippings during the fall.

Remember to dead-head, or lightly prune many flowering plants to encourage a new flush of blooms.

It is not too late to plant all those heat loving annuals like caladiums, vincas, celosia, Zinnias and Marigolds. They will require lots of extra water for the first few weeks, because you're planting them in August, but they will look good up until the first cold spell.

This is a good time to control nutgrass/nutsedge with a selective herbicide called Manage.

You can control Fall Webworms -- those that make their appearances in September – by treating the leaves of trees with liquid Bt (bascillius thuringeinsis). It targets only leaf-eating worms and caterpillars.

If Brownpatch was a problem in your turf last year, be prepared to start a monthly treatment of systemic fungicides as early as August.

If you have big Oak trees with thick canopies, consider having a tree company remove dead limbs and opening up the tree for air circulation, especially during hurricane season.

If you didn't do your June/July lawn fertilization, please don't do it now because it's too HOT. However, you can add an iron supplement if there is a general yellowing to the grass because of all the irrigation.

Some trees that are under heavy stress, will throw leaves as a defense mechanism.

Consider deep root feeding/watering of such trees. (See Trees Chapter for details)

If you're using an irrigation system, always water in the mornings to help prevent any potential fungal disease. Brownpatch spores love lots of moisture on nights where the low temperatures are in the 60s.

September Checklist

The biggest lesson to learn for the many transplants or new residents along the Gulf Coast (I'm talking "people" here) is to understand that September does not mean cooler weather here. If you remember that, it will save you a lot of aggravation.

Many nurseries and garden centers start having clearance sales. Many sales boast prices up to 75 percent off. It's a good time to stock up on bargain plants, considering that October is reputed to be the best month to plant things.

This is a big month for fall vegetable gardens. Tomatoes and peppers are easy to grow. Don't wait until the end of the month. They must be protected, however, from potential intense summer-like temperatures.

This is a good month to plant Chrysanthemums (Garden Mums) from potted plants to the landscape. They will give you immediate color in the autumn months.

Grub worms can be a problem, eating up the root systems of grass and newly planted flower beds. Try Triazicide as a replacement for Dursban and Diazinon, which are no longer available to the retail market.

Start building that compost pile with fall leaf accumulation.

Keep up your monthly Brownpatch control.

Despite the show of Pansies, and other cool season annuals, at garden centers, don't plant them until late October or early November. They will likely die if the soil temperature hasn't cooled enough.

Consider a fall pruning of Hybrid Tea and Floribunda Roses. You don't need to cut as much as you did in February, but more than the ever-so-light pruning of the summer.

October Checklist

Apply pre-emergent herbicides, especially the 2-in-1 formulas. By applying a pre-emergent now, you block Poa Anna and various broadleaf weeds like clover from popping up in January.

October is the perfect month to re-do or even start big landscape projects. October is historically the best month for establishing root systems of trees and shrubs before winter comes. By establishing them now, you will be rewarded with vibrant growth in spring.

It's bulb season. That means keep an eye out for all the bulb marts/shows/sales. Except for the bulbs that require refrigeration, most bulbs can go in the ground any time in October or November.

This is also considered the best month for dividing and moving bulbs and perennials, such as Lilies and Iris.

This is the perfect month to finally prune those Oleanders.

Do your Winterizer formulation for turfgrass fertilization. The most important number to remember in winterizers is the last number, the Potassium. It needs to be higher than 10. The nitrogen, the first number, shouldn't ever exceed 18.

If you have caladium bulbs and want to save them for next year, dig them up. Store these bulbs in a cool, dry location and make sure all the dirt is off of every part.

Stop feeding your roses.

If you like 10-15 onions, and you have a vegetable garden, this is the time to plant them. That's how they got their name, considering that the 15th of October is their optimum planting date.

Stay on the lookout for Brownpatch outbreaks, and keep up the monthly fungicide control.

November Checklist

Now you can plant those pansies and other cool season annuals. Incorporate any of the slow-release blooming plant foods into the planting hole and you won't have to worry about feeding them again for at least three months. If you did not do your winterizer fertilizer application, then do so NOW! Remember, it's never too late to do the right thing.

Cyclamens are the best cool season annual for shady situations. But you can try others like Snapdragons and Dianthus during the early winter months.

If you know a freeze is on the way, water the landscape plants thoroughly around the root zone. Since the ground never freezes along the Gulf Coast, it is one of the best ways to keep plants safe during colder weather.

Apply a layer of mulch for winter protection, weed prevention and overall aesthetics.

Falling leaves and pine needles make instant mulch for flower beds. There are some leaves that contain tannins that do not make for a good mulch material. Avoid leaves from Pecans, Live Oaks and Hickories as examples of those with too much tannin.

Don't forget to vote in elections the first Tuesday in November. (That's the most political I can ever get.)

Consider pinching back (dead-heading) garden mums. They will push out new blooms if you can eliminate most of the expired ones.

If you have a vegetable garden, consider picking green tomatoes right before any freeze. Fried Green Tomatoes or Chow Chow is a much better alternative than damage fruit.

Thanksgiving is considered the best time to start planting daffodils and narcissus.

Prepare to move Plumerias for forced winter dormancy.

December Checklist

Find the closest Christmas Tree Farm (www.TexasChristmasTrees.com) or choose-and-cut operation for your Christmas tree this year. It's an experience your kids will love, and you'll be getting a much fresher Christmas tree.

Gardening gifts are great for the gardening enthusiast at this time of the year. pH meters, hand trowel kits, Bionic gardening gloves, bird feeders and gardening books always make great gifts for the "green thumbs" in your family.

Be on the lookout for Scale insects on Hollies and many other evergreen shrubs. Since we aren't out in the garden as much, unnoticed populations can build up quickly.

If you haven't applied that protective layer of mulch in November, do so NOW!

If there is little rain from Mother Nature in December, don't forget to water the plants and the grass. Soak them both deeply because even though there is little "active" growth on the shrubs and trees, their root systems are still very much in need of moisture.

While January is best, you can start thinking about major pruning jobs on large trees.

Don't forget there are many other cool season annual options out there besides Pansies – such as Calendula, Sweet Alyssum, Stocks, Dianthus, Snapdragons, Ornamental Kale and Ornamental Cabbage. Cyclamen are great for shady areas.

Protect plants from freeze damage with Frost Covers, sheets and blankets. Don't just use tarps or plastic.

If you cover things at night, and if the temperatures are above 32 degrees during the day, you need to remove freeze protection, to allow for air and sunshine.

If you have a vegetable garden, now is the time to plant unusual Cole crops like Mustard Greens, Turnips, Leeks and Green Onions.

Be on the lookout for Amaryllis sales. They also make great potted gift plants for housewarmings or holiday parties.

If you need to transplant Azaleas, December is considered one of the best months to actually move them.

If you get Bonsai plants for holiday gifts, remember to keep them outdoors to grow and indoors to show. They are actual dwarf trees, so they need air and sunshine.

Get ready to plant the refrigerated bulbs. The last week of December is considered the best month to start planting Tulips, Crocus and Hyacinth.

About the Author

Randy Lemmon is the host of Houston's GardeLine radio program, on NewsRadio 740 KTRH. Randy has been doing GardenLine in one capacity or another since December of 1995, for all three of the now Clear Channel AM stations – KTRH, KBME & KPRC. When Randy took over GardenLine he replaced long-time Houston radio veteran, and GardenLine originator, Bill Zak. Randy's program is now heard Saturdays and Sundays on 740 KTRH from 6 a.m. to 10 a.m.

Before doing radio in Houston, Randy was the Communications Specialists for the College of Agriculture and Life Sciences at Texas A&M University. Prior to that, Randy served as Assistant Director or Radio and Television Services for the Texas Farm Bureau in Waco.

Although it may appear Randy has been involved in Agriculture and Horticulture exclusively, he also served as a producer for the R.C. Slocum Coach's Show in the early 90s. And Randy was a sports reporter/anchor for KAMU-TV in Bryan-College Station as well as KCEN-TV in Waco.

Randy earned a B.S. in Journalism from Texas A&M University in 1984. Then he earned a Master's in Agricultural Education in '95 while working for Texas A&M's College of Agriculture and Life Sciences.

Randy and his wife Yvonne have two children and split a lot of their time between their home in Cypress, Texas and their place in Galveston, Texas as well. Randy says he gets the biggest sense of pride in his job when people call and email him about how he saved their lawns, gave them the best looking landscape on the block or saved them lots of money in doing things themselves.

He has a side business, known as **Randy Lemmon Consulting,** where he evaluates and makes recommendations in full reports for both homeowners and commercial sites.

You can always ask more questions and get even more gardening information at Randy's website... www.RandyLemmon.com

Invite Randy Lemmon to Your
Next Group Function

Randy Lemmon can be scheduled for book signings as well as appearances. He is available for a variety of speaking engagements from garden clubs to civic associations to home owner's association meetings. He entertains audiences, big or small, as an emcee, keynote speaker or simply for intimate Q&A sessions.

For more information on Randy's availability and speaking fees, please send an email to the link below. Put the words Speaker Request in the subject line. randylemmon@clearchannel.com Or, leave a detailed message at 713-212-8126

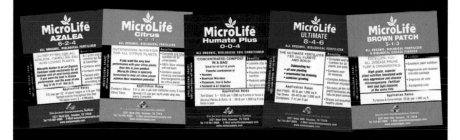

the perfect fit.
naturally!

IDEAL SOIL FOR RAISED BEDS!

Soil Mender
ALL-NATURAL
Stimulate
for all lawns and gardens

Soil Mender
Rose Food

Soil Mender
Tomato & Vegetable Food

Soil Mender
Raised Bed Mix
organic topsoil, composted cotton burrs, cotton, expanded shale, lava sand, granite sand, basalt, humate, montmorillonite, & diatomaceous earth
Ideal soil for raised bed & container gardening

ORGANIC
HU-MAX
HEARTY & RICH SOIL SOLUTIONS
1-1-1
TURF SOIL BUILDER

Soil Mender
Foliar Plus

Soil Mender
Foliar Plus

explore a full range of natural garden products

All of which are formulated with one goal in mind - to build
healthy, living soil that produces thriving plants. An extensive
variety of products ensures that anyone's needs will be met.
Plus, these safe and simple product solutions are backed with
the quality that the Soil Mender® name represents. Growing
naturally has never been easier!

Soil Mender®
Products

www.soilmender.com
3071 Hwy. 86 | Tulia, TX 79088
800-441-2498   Fax: 806-627-4277